St. Patrick's School

South Farnborough

A Potted History 1886 ~ 1968

By

Bryan Hoskyns

2014

Published by Bryan Hoskyns

© Bryan Hoskyns 2014

978-0-9928656-0-3

Printed by

Dollin Press Services Ltd.

Whitchurch, Hampshire, RG2 7BB

Front cover: St. Patrick's School main building

Back cover: St. Patrick's School Rear building.

Contents

List of Illustrations	p4
Acknowledgements	p6
Preface	p8
Prologue	p10
Early Days	p11
Miss Alice Crowley	p15
The Arrival of the Salesian Fathers	p19
The Death of Father Riordan	p21
The Following Years	p22
The First Word War and Beyond	p27
Pro Ecclesia et Pontifice	p31
A New Dawn	p32
A Time for Change	p38
The Second Would War	p40
Post War	p44
The 1950s	p47
A New Secondary-modern	p57
The Infants and Juniors	p59
The New St. Patricks	p61
Former Teachers	p62

List of Illustrations

1	School Photograph 1958	Author	p8
2	School Children 1890	Diocese of Portsmouth	p12
3	School Chapel Sketch	Maeve Moon	p13
4	Main School Building	Our Lady Help of Christians	p13
5	Map of South Farnborough	Farnborough Library	p14
6	St. Patrick	St. Michael's Abbey Press	p18
7	St. John Bosco	Wikipedia	p19
8	St. Maria Mazzarello	Wikipedia	p20
9	Father Riordan	Diocese of Portsmouth	p21
10	First Communion 1923	Mary Rush nee Hunt	p28
11	First Communion 1928	Mary Rush nee Hunt	p29
12	May Day 1935	Mary Rush nee Hunt	p29
13	Alice Crowley	Mary Rush nee Hunt	p30
14	Badge of the Knights	Knights of St. Columba	p33
15	A New Classroom	Our Lady Help of Christians	p34
16	First Communion 1933	Renee Newcombe nee Tottle	p35
17	First Communion 1935	Renee Newcombe nee Tottle	p35
18	May Day 1935	Renee Newcombe nee Tottle	p36
19	Sister Frances	Salesian Sisters, Cowley	p37
20	Sister Marie	Jane Steel nee Still	p38
21	Badge of C. W. L.	Catholic Woman's League	p39
22	Sister Patricia	Jane Still nee Steel	p43

23 First Communion 1947	Jane Steel nee Still	p45
24 Teachers and Pupils 1948	Mark O'Sullivan	p46
25 Disused Army Hut	Rushmoor Borough Council.	p47
26 Proposed Wash Room	Rushmoor Borough Council	p48
27 The Festival of Britain	Jane Steel nee Still	p49
28 Temporary Classroom	Rushmoor Borough Council	p50
29 Group Photograph, 1955	Greta Hewings nee Fearon	p51
30 Sunday School Tuck Box	Margaret Bartlett nee Morris	p52
31 Sunday School Pavilion	Margaret Bartlett nee Morris	p52
32 Mr. Lashley's Class, 1955	Mr. Lashley	p53
33 Football Team 1953/54	Alan Botley	p53
34 Plan of the School Grounds	Rushmoor Borough Council	p54
35 Mr. Lashley's Class, 1958	Mr. Lashley	p56
36 All Hallows School	All Hallows, Weybourne	p57
37 All Hallows School	All Hallows, Weybourne	p58
38 Original 'Arched' Entrance	Our Lady Help of Christians	p59
39 Folding Partition	Our Lady Help of Christians	p59
40 Teachers and Staff	Our Lady Help of Christians	p60
41 Avenue Road School	Author	p61
42 Cup Winners 1954/55	Alan Botley	p64
43 League Winners 1954/55	Alan Botley	p65
44 School Class, Late 1950s	Mr. Lashley	p67
45 School Class Early 1960s	Mr. Lashley	p67

Acknowledgements

Aldershot Library, Aldershot News, All Hallows School, Weybourne.

Catholic Herald, Catholic National Library, Downside Abbey Library,

Farnborough Library, Catholic Women's League, Farnborough.

Diocese of Portsmouth, Hampshire Record Office,

National Archives, Kew. Rushmoor Borough Council,

Salesian Sisters, Cowley. Salesian Sisters, Liverpool.

St. Joseph's School, Aldershot.

The author also wishes to thank the following:

Thomas Atkins, Margaret Bartlett nee Morris, Alan Botley, Diane Carver,

Paul Costen, Sister Ann Darwin, Trevor Dooner, Patrick Duane,

Robert Eeckelaers, Gretta Hewings nee Fearon, Pamela Fontana,

Doctor Val Fontana, Sister Eileen Fowley, Reginald Hunt,

Audrey King nee Dixon, John Lashley, Theresa Loader nee Reed,

Stella Loten nee Doona, Thelmer Lotton nee Doona,

Patricia Lyons nee Allen, Tony Martin, Renee Newcombe nee Tottle,

Kevin, O'Brien, Patricia Pierce, Arthur Powell, Catherine Raggett,

Mary Rush nee Hunt, Robert Ryan, David Rymill, Sister Kathleen Scullion,

Jane Steel nee Still, George Still, Mary Williams nee Doherty,

Sister Bridie Woods.

~~~

With the intention of producing a second edition at a future date, the author would like to hear from anybody who has any additional information or photographs of the school.

I dedicate this book to

former teachers, pupils and staff

of St. Patrick's School

Peabody Road, Farnborough.

Preface

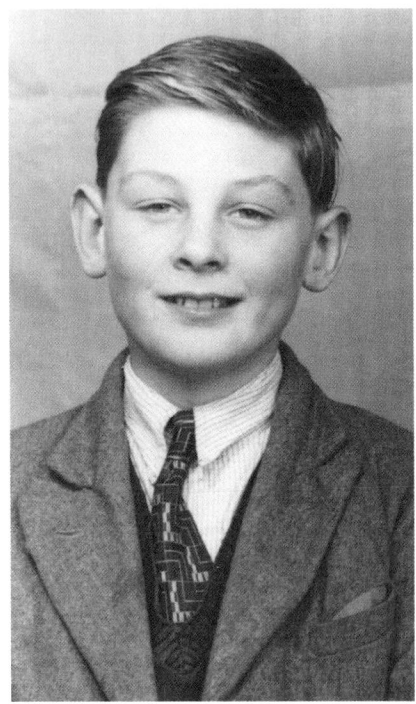

**Bryan Hoskyns
School photograph 1958**

Although we lived in North Farnborough, my parents, being of the Catholic faith sent me to St. Patrick's Roman Catholic School, Peabody Road, South Farnborough, which I attended from 1949 to 1959. The Headmistress during those years was Sister Marie Ranner FMA, who conducted a strict and disciplined school for 30 years.

The church-style building consisted of four classrooms, of which two were divided by a folding partition. It also had a modest bell tower and each morning, Sister Marie, tugging on a long rope, would ring this bell to announce that the school was open. She would also ring a hand bell at the morning, lunchtime and afternoon playtimes, and if you were brave enough, and asked her very nicely, she would let you ring it at the end of one of those playtimes.

The school was attended by infant, junior and senior pupils and in all there were seven classrooms. However, it wasn't enough to accommodate the ten years of schooling. In many instances, this problem was solved by pupils spending two years in the same classroom. That is to say, two streams occupied one classroom which, in some instances, could be as many as fifty or more pupils.

Religious instruction took place on a regular basis and much effort was put into learning the catechism by rote, enabling a child to receive their First Holy Communion. This took place in the church of Our Lady Help of Christians, Queens Road, and those taking their First Communion were dressed in white. Having received their first communion the communicants, together with the rest of the congregation, assembled outside of the church in the Salesian grounds. Singing hymns, a procession then took a route out of the grounds and proceeded into Sherbourne Road. They then followed a route via Queens Road, turning right along Peabody Road to the corner of Reading Road where the procession then again turned right and, going through a Lynch gate, re-entered the Salesian grounds. Group photographs were then taken of those proud boys and girls.

Those children having received Holy Communion then attended Mass once a month on a Friday morning at Our Lady Help of Christians. Walking out of the back gate 'crocodile fashion' they proceeded along the un-adopted Sherborne Road to attend a service and partake of Holy Communion: fasting from the previous night was mandatory.

Another important event was the sacrament of Confirmation. It was conferred on a child at the age of fourteen at Mass, the service being taken by the Bishop of Portsmouth. During the service the Bishop anoints the child making the sign of the cross on their forehead with Holy Chrism oil. The person anointed also takes the name of their chosen saint.

The school had three temporary classrooms: an old, black wooden hut housed classrooms 1 and 2, while classroom 3 was of modern, prefabricated construction having larger windows. Immediately outside the old wooden hut were three air raid shelters that had been built in 1939; they were covered in grass and, as you can imagine, we were forbidden to play on them.

A netball pitch was marked-out on the playground which gave the girls plenty of practice of their shooting skills. Skipping and throwing tennis balls against the wall was also popular.

In the corner of the playground was a Tuck shop, not least to tempt those children who had as little as a farthing, a halfpenny, a penny, tuppence or a thru'penny-bit.

A row of sturdy oak trees partitioned the main playground from a dirt playground where occasionally a shallow lake would form in the winter months! Here the boys played football, cricket and other adventurous games. There was also a climbing frame close to the boundary fence for pupils to exercise on.

On the north side was the slaughter house where balls of all types would often end up, and it was a brave pupil indeed, who would risk going out of the back gate into Sherbourne Road, to sneak into the slaughter house and retrieve the ball. Woe betide anyone caught trying to do so!

There was no gymnasium, and when it came to football, cricket and baseball, both juniors and seniors would be marched, crocodile-fashion to Boundary Road playing fields where the annual Sports Day also took place.

When it came to swimming, the juniors attended the Puddle which was also in Boundary Road. It had two outdoor pools, one shallow and one sloping deeper towards the far end. Swimming lessons as such weren't given, you just taught yourself. However, when you became a senior pupil, you attended the Army Command Baths.

I played for the St. Patrick's under 15 football team, which was in the Aldershot and Farnborough Schools League, our colours being green and yellow shirts with white shorts. One of our best performances was in a cup match against the Farnborough Grammar School which resulted in a one-all draw. Unfortunately, in the replay at home, we lost four nil!

School outings were also arranged and those that I went on were: an agricultural show near Winchester; a boat ride on the river Thames at Windsor and, most memorably, a visit to Wembley Stadium to watch a schoolboy international football match between England and Germany, the result being a draw, one all.

Two other school outings I remember with much nostalgia were to the Scala Cinema in Camp Road. The first was to see a film of the Coronation of Queen Elizabeth II with its glittering pomp and ceremony. The second was to see Edmund Hillary and Sherpa Tensing's conquest of Mount Everest. The two coming so close together, were memorable occasions which everyone in the land cheered and rejoiced in.

Concerts were organised and took place in the playground until a new hall was built in Peabody Road. It was a vast improvement, not only for the school, but for the audience as well, who now had the comfort of an in-door venue, while we, the actors, had both the anxiety of 'stage-fright', and the excitement of performing on a real stage. Needless to say, it gave the concerts a new dimension and was even more popular with the parents.

In my final year, on the last day of term, my class teacher, Mrs. Porter, permitted us to play pop records. Not only that, she also allowed us to dance as well! We then had a break outside and while doing so, heard the melodious sounds of the piano being played. Slowly, we crept back in to find Mrs. Porter playing classical music. There was a momentary pause in the music and we all clapped. Unfortunately, she hadn't quite completed the piece and said, 'I don't mind you all clapping, but please wait until I've finished.' The music, dancing and jollity continued for a while. Eventually we were allowed to leave, and saying our goodbyes to Mrs. Porter, and one and all, the class slowly drifted away in dribs and drabs.

Teachers I remember during my time at the school: Mrs. Pugh; Sister Patricia; Mrs Birch; Mrs. Vernon; Miss Keenan; Mr Lashley; Mr Powell and Mrs Porter.

Bryan Hoskyns

*****

Prologue

I think it must have been sometime back in the early 1970's I'd gone to North Camp, South Farnborough, and for whatever reason, found myself reminiscing about my school days at St. Patrick's, so I decided to take a walk down Peabody Road. However, as I approached, all I could see was a terrace of three new houses. How disappointed I was, but all I could do was to retrace my steps and put it to the back of my mind.

It wasn't until 1993 that an idea entered my mind of finding a photograph of the old school; but where to start? The first thing that came into my mind was to try and contact my old Head Teacher, Sister Marie Ranner. It seemed a good idea and, anyway, I had nothing to lose. The obvious place to start was the Salesian College, and that's where I headed to make enquiries. Much to my delight I was informed that Sister Marie had retired and was living in Streatham, London. I also found out that she had made plans to attend a church service at Our Lady Help of Christians, Farnborough, sometime during the summer, so I quickly made arrangements to meet her there.

On the day I joined the service and afterwards met up with Sister Marie. It was a lovely day and we sat in the Salesian gardens. Although it was well over 30 years since we'd met, we talked enthusiastically about old times at the school.

Towards the end of our conversations I asked if she had a photograph of the school. Alas, she said that she'd mislaid most of her belongings, but she would look anyway and let me know. We then had our photograph taken in the gardens and soon afterwards she returned to Streatham.

I kept in touch for a short while, visiting her at Streatham whenever I was in the area. Of course the elusive photo never surfaced. Even so, I felt privileged to have met her again, and very much enjoyed our time together.

Fifteen years later, with a little more determination, I again took up the cudgel of researching the old school in a vain hope of finding some photographs, not realising the angst and frustration I'd experience along the way. It would take me quite some time, but time was now on my side: I contacted the Salesian College, enquired at Farnborough Abbey, phoned the Diocese of Portsmouth and the Winchester Record Office too. I searched through old books and newspapers and also put a request on the internet! Still those photographs eluded me. However, I wasn't to be put off and continued my search. Along the way, I gradually began to unearth various interesting articles about the school, mainly from old local newspapers, the most interesting being the date of the opening of the school, which was 1890. It was during this period it dawned on me that I would like to compile a history of the school.

In the meantime, I continued my search for that elusive photograph and, eventually, I got what I'd been searching for, for so long. I'd contacted Robert Eeckaers, the editor of Our Lady Help of Christians' Contact magazine. He agreed to search their records and managed to locate, not one, but six photographs of the school: two were of the building; three were of the classrooms, the last one showing the teachers and staff. The photographs were not dated, but are believed to have been taken in 1965 when the new school opened in Avenue Road for the junior pupils. And, believe it or not, the six photos that Robert Eeckaers sent to me just happened to arrive through my letter box on St Patrick's Day! And can you imagine just how delighted I was? However, my elation was short lived; I soon found out that the school log books had gone missing. It meant that I would now have to look elsewhere to discover the school's history. But, given time, it eventually turned out to be a good thing. It made me even more determined to discover my goal. And over a long period of time, searching through many documents and sources, it eventually led me to a varied and interesting story …

*****

Early Days

With the influx of the Army into Aldershot, the Catholic Church of St. Joseph had been well established along with a school of the same name. Attention was then focused on Farnborough, which had received a similar amount of Army personnel, and where there were estimated to be ninety to one hundred Catholic children, who had no such facility other than a Sunday school that was being held at the Garrison church of St Louis under the jurisdiction of the Army Chaplain, Joseph Corbett.

Up until 1886 Catholic children had been using the Wesleyan Methodist School, Lynchford Road, South Farnborough, for their schooling, so the need for a Catholic school had become acute. Bishop Virtue of the Diocese of Portsmouth pointed out that the children, living as they did in the Parish, ought to have a Catholic school provided for them. He also pointed out that it was important that the children were given the opportunity to study religious education in order to receive the sacraments while growing up.

The project was given to Fr. Riordan, a much respected priest of St. Joseph's Church, who found himself faced with financial difficulties from the very beginning. It would continue for the rest of his active life, both in Aldershot and Farnborough, which proved in the event to be a period of eighteen years.

Firstly, he alone was given the enormous tasks of trying to pay current expenses of the mission out of small receipts. Secondly, there was the debt on the church to be paid off. Thirdly, there was the need to enlarge the schools as the years passed by. In addition he had also been given the task of establishing a school-chapel in South Farnborough when funds were very scarce. Undaunted, he set about the task and, with little money, managed to persuade the War Department to rent out 'an old wooden hut' that had already been marked for demolition, its location being just inside the military area of the North Camp.

Fr. Riordan then set about employing a Catholic certificated mistress and assistant. Once employed, permission was then given from the Education Department for the school to be certified. The school was eventually opened in November 1886. The hut was in use for four years and, according to Government Inspectors: "The children had done well in their examinations." Progress was also made in religious knowledge and merited special praise by the Diocesan Inspector.

Having established a temporary school in the North Camp for Catholic children, Fr. Riordan was then able to turn his attention to the building of a new school in the area. Fortunately for Fr. Riordan the Duke of Norfolk stepped in and purchased land in Peabody Road, South Farnborough. This left Fr. Riordan with an enormous task on his hands: how to raise no less than £700 for the building of the school. One of the ways he set about accomplishing the feat was to raise a Suppliart.

Children Suppliart 1890

Please send a postal order for two or three shillings or a few postage stamps to our Priest, Father Riordan, to help him to build us a school. We are being turned out, as you see, from our present one, and we are looking to him to build us a new one. He says that as he has not got the money he had us Children beg.
Won't you help him and us?
    We are
        Yours sincerely,
            THE CHILDREN OF NORTH CAMP
            CATHOLIC SCHOOL.

School children outside the Army hut, 1890. Owing to damage to the original photograph it has been digitally enhanced with some duplication of children.

In response, money was raised from the parishioners of Aldershot and Farnborough to the amount of £200, leaving the larger amount of £500 outstanding, the majority of which was carried over until 1901 when the Salesian Fathers came to the town. Fr. Riordan was then able to build exactly what had been needed for so long: an Elementary School-Chapel.

The school was opened in 1890, consisting of mixed classes. Unfortunately, a shortage of priests meant that the Chapel could not be used. A solution was found when Fr. Riordan approached Her Imperial Majesty the Empress Eugenie at Farnborough Hill, who had founded a Priory and Abbey at North Farnborough. The Empress also constructed a Mausoleum beneath the Abbey for her late husband Napoleon III, Emperor of France, and their son the Prince Imperial, both of whom were buried in the Imperial crypt. Norbertine Canons, who came from Storrington Priory in 1887 to administer services at the Abbey, agreed to provide mass at the School-Chapel each Sunday.

Fr. Riordan then handed over the School and chapel to the charge of the Prior of the Norbertines. The school, which most likely didn't have a title at that time, was then given the name of St. Norbert after their founder, St Norbert: The Canons were also known as Premonstratensians, the Order having been established in Premontre, Northern France, in 1120.

~~~

An artist's impression of the school-chapel based on government documents dated 1889 - 1891.

The number of pupils attending the school quickly outgrew the school's capacity to provide space for them and in March 1891 an extension to the south side of the school was approved. It was to add an extra classroom for infant pupils, increasing the number of places to 128 children. Construction was completed sometime between 1891 and 1893.

This view shows the extension to the main building including a dormer window, two wash rooms at right-angles to each other and a bell tower.

This is the only known photograph of the front of the school, which was taken in the 1960s before closure.

~~~

Farnborough Parish Minutes

Having successfully opened the school in the winter of 1890, Father Riordan's plans for the extension, which were approved by the Education Department, were then looked at by the surveyor of the Farnborough Parish Committee. The following notes were recorded in the Farnborough Parish Minutes book of 1889 to 1892 as quoted on 29th. May 1891:

Plans of new schools for Rev. E. Riordan were received and it appearing that the schools have already been commenced. The surveyor was instructed to see that the buildings are being constructed in all respects according to bylaws & the plans deposited.

~~~

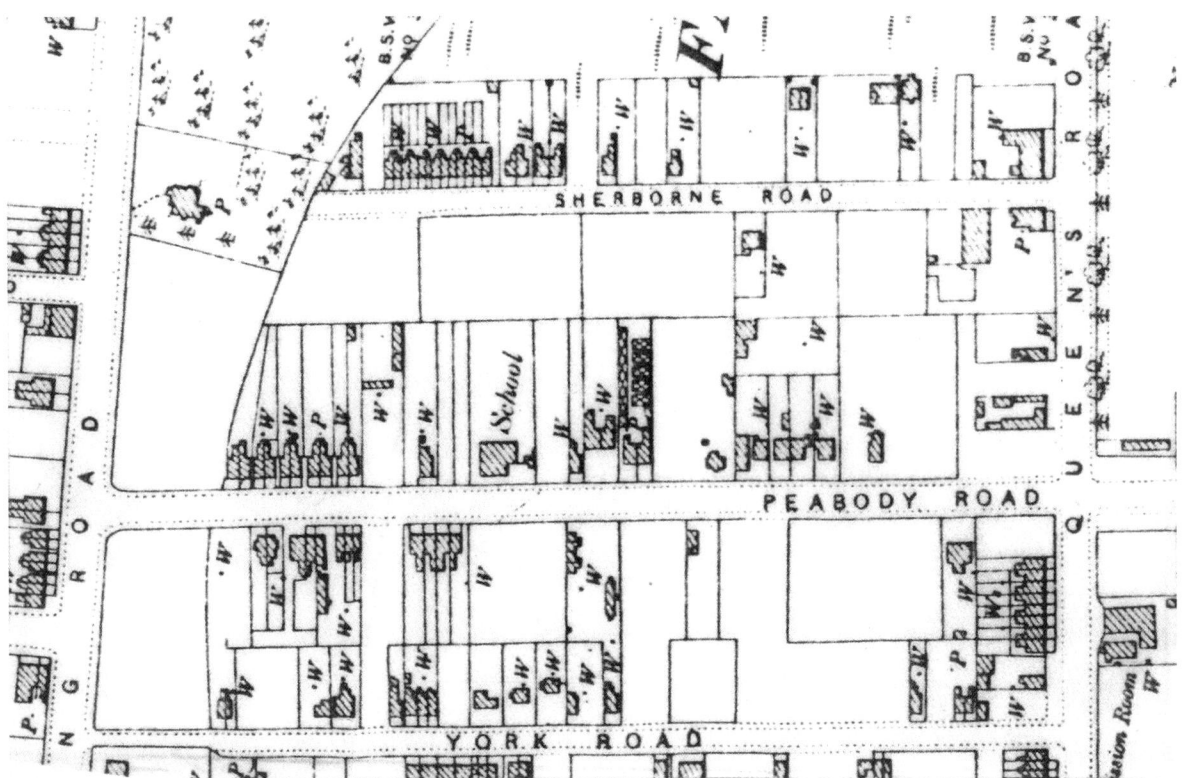

Ordinance Survey map of South Farnborough showing Peabody Road in the 1890s. The extension to the school is to the right and the toilet block is opposite.

*****

Miss Alice Crowley

In February 1893 Miss Alice Crowley was appointed Headmistress of St. Norbert's and, haven taken charge of the mixed class, she would prove to be a revelation.

Born in Brompton and educated at St. Winifred's Convent, Cale Street, Chelsea, Miss Crowley became a Pupil Teacher there at the age of fourteen. She then went on to pass the Queen's Scholarship Examination in 1885 and spent the two following years as a student at the Sacred Heart, Wandsworth. After leaving college she was appointed assistant mistress at Grays School, Essex and then went on to become head teacher at Tooley-street Catholic School, Bermondsey, South London.

Interestingly, her next teaching post was to take her to Lancashire where she was appointed headmistress at Chapel End Elementary School, Billinge. It was after this that she took up the post at St. Norbert's and, by the following year, had organised a concert by the children, which took place in the school. As reported by *Sheldrakes Military Gazette on the 2nd. June 1894*

CONCERT AT FARNBOROUGH

A very successful concert was held at the Catholic Schools, Peabody Road, Farnborough, on Wednesday, May 23 rd.

The school was filled to its utmost capacity with an appreciative audience. A string band, under the conductorship of Mr. Geo. Thomas, opened the proceedings with the overture "Chevalier Breton." The boys of the school then went through the musical drill in a soldier-like manner. Great credit is due to Corpl. Harrington (Lincolns), who trained them. An operetta, "Fairy Queen," by the children, was next on the programme. The children performed their different parts in a way which showed that they had been really well looked after – each one of them knowing their part to perfection – reflecting the highest praise on Miss Crowley, the schoolmistress ...

~~~

The Benedictines

Following a disagreement with the Empress in 1895, the Norbertine Monks left Farnborough and returned to Storrington Priory. The Empress then solicited Benedictine monks in Solesmes, France, who were known for their scholarly writing and traditional Gregorian chants, to take over the running of the Priory at Farnborough. They did so, on the premise that the Abbey be given over to them. The Empress agreed and the monks then took full responsibility for both the Priory and chapel-mausoleum, which together formed St. Michael's Abbey. However the monks declined to carry out the Sunday services at the school-chapel leaving the duties for the care of Catholics in Farnborough, once again, back in the hands of Fr. Riordan. Unfortunately, because of his commitments, it was impossible for him to do so. The only solution was to engage another priest, and Fr. Albert George Clark was sent as an assistant, his duties being to provide Mass on Sunday at the School-chapel and to manage the school affairs, which continued until August 1898. Fr. Clark was then replaced by Fr. James Doran; his duties were to continue to serve the parish of Farnborough which included the provision of Mass at the school-chapel.

~~~

Mary Parish

In September 1895 Miss Mary Parish, who had previously taught at St. Joseph's Roman Catholic school in Aldershot, was appointed Assistant Headmistress at St. Norbert's, and took charge of the infants. At this time the average attendance was 100 and, together, Alice Crowley and Mary Parish were successful in their efforts in educating the children. Three years later, in February 1898, the school received a good report from Her Majesty's Inspectors that resulted in Government grants being made in compliance with the Elementary School's Education Act of 1891, as reported by the *Aldershot News*:

Her Majesty's Inspector of Schools paid his second visit under Article 84 (b) of the Day School Code to the Catholic School, Peabody Road, on Tuesday morning. He examined the children in arithmetic, dictation, reading, geography, needlework, and drill, and expressed himself very pleased with the result. There are now a few vacancies both in the infant and in the mixed department for new scholars.

~~~

The Hillside Convent

In 1886, Mother Duval, the Mother Superior General of the Congregation of Christian Education in Argentan, France, came to England. Her mission was to establish a convent specifically for the daughters of British Army Officers. After much searching for a suitable property Mother Duval set her heart on one particular house in Farnborough. Though small, it was adequate for their needs with modest gardens giving way to a backdrop of pine trees. Its name was Hillside. The property was acquired in the spring of 1889 and opened as a school on the 15th. May that year.

Located towards the top of Star Hill, Farnborough Road, it was to become the Hillside Convent, where, during the turn of the century, fetes were organised to raise funds, not only for St. Norbert's school, but also for a Boy's Orphanage in Queens Road.

In 1898, Mother Deplanck the first Mother Superior at the Hillside Convent, invited children from St. Norbert's School for afternoon tea, as reported by *Sheldrakes Military Gazette:*

CATHOLIC SCHOOL FARNBOROUGH

The children attending the Catholic School, Peabody Road, Farnborough, were kindly entertained at tea by the Rev. Mother Superior of Hillside Convent, on Friday last. They arrived about two in the afternoon and after an hour or so had been devoted to various amusements in the beautiful grounds of the Convent, sat down to an excellent tea under the shade of the pine trees. After tea they once more betook themselves to various pastimes until 6:30, when they dispersed, having spent a thoroughly enjoyable day.

The Rev. E. Riordan and the Rev. A. G. Clarke (corresponding manager of the school) were present during the afternoon.

~~~

1899 Concert

A varied and extensive programme of events was performed at the school on the 27th December 1899, by both adults and children alike, as reported by *Sheldrakes Military Gazette:*

CONCERT AT THE CATHOLIC SCHOOL

... a very successful children's entertainment or concert was given at the Peabody Road Schools, on Wednesday evening, the arrangements having been in the very capable hands of Miss Crowley, the Governess of the larger school, and of Miss Parish, head of the infants department. The schoolroom had been made very bright and picturesque by these ladies, with the help of the young folk, flags and bunting being lavishly introduced, whilst the stage itself was quite a natty affair. The programme was a very well arranged one, and there was not a single item that was included therein but what gave every pleasure and satisfaction to the company which assembled. The programme opened with the overture "Le Sac de Come," by Mdlle. Kuntz The kindness of this talented instrumentalist was greatly appreciated and it is needless to say that her effort was accorded the heartiest of applause. Mr. Buckmaster followed with a well rendered tenor song "Queen of the earth," and he too, well deserved the ovation that was his. A recital "Hang up Babies Stocking," by the infants was very good, as was also the part song "Lullaby, "by the elder scholars. The pole drill by the boys was smart to a degree, and the infants afforded much pleasure in their action song "The Merry Gypsies," The elder scholars displayed the result of much careful and successful tuition in their part song " Merry Times," and the infants recital of "The Coach," won applause. In their round "The Bells," the elder scholars were again successful, and the action song "Soldiers of the Queen," by the infants carried the enthusiasm of the audience to quite a high pitch. The infants having given a bell drill display, Mdlle. Chevalier sang with guitar accomplishment, and gave way to Mdlle. Kuntz in the overture, "Valse de Durand," both being all that could be desired. Mdlle. Chevalier also sang "La Bateliere," with excellent effect. Then came on other contributions, all well rendered, from the elder girls, including a round, "Wind, Gentle Evergreen," very pretty; a part song, "In the Dusk of the Twilight," and part song. "The Battle Eve," and "I Know a Bank," whilst the infants gave the action song "Eight Little Mothers" (very good), hoop drill, by girls; action song, "The Japanese Fan," infants; a duet, "The Cat's Duet," by Misses Norah Dilley, and Daisy Lugdon, caused much laughter, and Mddle. Chevalier put a capital finish to the programme by singing "Le Depurt de I'Etudeiant," then God Save the Queen" was sung.

~~~

Pupil Teacher

Alice Elley, aged 14, joined the staff in January 1899 as a Pupil Teacher to assist Miss Crowley and Miss Parish with the day-to-day running of the school.

~~~

A New Name for the School

St. Patrick

A momentous decision was made in 1900 when the school authorities decided to change the name of the school. Needless to say, it would have to be named after a saint, but which one? There must have been much deliberation about the matter and many suggestions would have been put forward to members of the school management committee. As we now know, they chose St. Patrick, the patron saint of Ireland. The first reference of their decision can be found in the *Catholic Directory* of that year.

St. Patrick was born in AD 387 and became a Christian Missionary during the 5th. century. He was ordained a Bishop by Pope Celestine and was successful in setting up hundreds of small churches in Ireland, and also converting the Celtic pagan population to Christianity.

~~~

In June 1901 the school received a favourable report which praised Alice Crowley and Mary Parish as reported by *Sheldrakes Military Gazette*:

FARNBOROUGH RC SCHOOL

It will be gratifying to parents of scholars and to well-wishers of the above schools to learn that the annual report of H. M. Inspector has been a most favourable one, calculated to give the greatest encouragement to all concerned in the management of the schools.

The following extracts from the report will doubtless be of interest.

Mixed School:- "The school is in a better state than last year. The class work is well done.

Infant Class: - "The infants are working very uncomfortably, and the only wonder is that they do so well.

The grants, per head, earned by the children of the mixed department are as follows.

Principal grant 12s. 6d., maximum, 14s; Discipline and organisation, 1s 6d.,maximum; Class subject. Geography, 2s.maximum; Singing by note, 1s. maximum; Needlework (girls) 1s. maximum; Drawing (boys) 1s. 9d. maximum: Infants class, fixed grant 9s. maximum; Variable grant, 6s. maximum; Needlework 1s. maximum; Singing by note 1s., Maximum.

It will thus be seen that the maximum grant has been gained in all the subjects of education, and great credit is due to the scholars for their attention to lessons, also to Miss. A. Crowley, head mistress of mixed department and to Miss M. Parish, mistress of infant class, who by their untiring efforts have achieved these successful results and such high official recognition.

*****

The Arrival of the Salesian Fathers

St. John Bosco

The Salesian Institution was founded at Valdocco near Turin where a school was opened in 1845 by St. John Bosco, through charitable works in order to care for young and poor children. Several more schools were then opened in Italy.

During the following years the institute began to expand abroad. Houses were opened in France in 1875, Argentina 1876, Spain in 1880 and Brazil in 1883. Eventually, a house was established in England at Battersea, South London, in 1887 where a college was built in 1895 for young boys aged eleven to eighteen.

In December 1901 Bishop Cahill made his first visitation of Aldershot. Debts were mounting and he discussed the future of the mission with Fr. Riordan. However, it was during a stay at the Diocese of Southwark that Bishop Cahill got the idea of employing the Salesian Fathers for the care of orphan boys.

One of his first tasks was to make better provision for a Male Orphanage at Farnborough. He later said that it was Canon St. John who suggested the calling in of the help of the Salesian Fathers. Fr. Riordan was in agreement and, consequently, he was relieved of his duties in Farnborough.

Arrangements were made and the Salesians took charge, buying up an old tinplate factory in Queens Road and adapting it for use as an Orphanage school. A church was then built adjacent to it, and was given the name 'Our Lady Help of Christians'. It was completed, and opened in 1902. Subsequently, the chapel in Peabody Road was no longer required. The Salesians also took charge of St. Patrick's school and were charged with looking after the pastoral needs of Catholics living in Farnborough. The first Fathers to arrive were: Fr. Ernest Marsh, Rector; Fr. Gregory Domanski, his assistant, and Fr. William Kelly, who was appointed Army Chaplain of the North Camp. By 1903, all three were appointed to the School Committee by the trustees of St. Patrick's.

A Catholic committee was formed with the intention to support a Salesian committee in a combined effort to erase the debt of St. Patrick's school and to help fund the Salesian Orphanage, both of which were voluntary aided. To achieve this, social events were organised, the first being a Café Chantant and Fancy Fair, which was held in the Hillside Convent School grounds, Farnborough in June 1903. Concerts and social events were also organised and held at the school in Peabody Road until 1906 when the more spacious Farnborough Town Hall was preferred.

~~~

In March 1904, the *Aldershot News* reported a most successful entertainment:

TO HELP ORPHANS

The children of the Catholic Schools at Farnborough gave a most successful entertainment in the Schoolroom on Wednesday evening. There was a packed audience, and as half those who came were unable to obtain admittance; it was decided to repeat the performance on the following night. Every item was given with marked intelligence and much humour. The pretty unconscious grace of the performers in the dances and action songs was particularly pleasing, and the arrangements reflected great credit on the organisers.

The opening choruses "Sweet and Low," and "The Nightingales' Trill" were sung by the senior boys and girls, the blending of the youthful voices being very harmonious. The senior girls gave in a charming manner the action songs "Three Modest Quakeresses," A. Powell, W. Elley and M. Lewington taking the chief parts, "Flowery Garlands," in which wreaths of flowers were gracefully introduced, and "The Daffodils." The children taking part in the last song wore frocks which simulated the flowers they represented. The dresses were of yellow gauze over white, falling from neck pieces of green, worn with wreaths of daffodils. Each song was followed by a limelight tableau. The senior boys gave evidence of specially good training. In the action song "The Lads in Blue," all wore white sailor suits, and the commander was in full rig with telescope complete; they performed the Flag Drill and the Hornpipe in splendid style. The tableau following was well grouped, and very effective. The infants gave in a quaint way the action songs "The Sailors," and the "Merry Little Gipsies, also the Cantata "The Jacks," which was very amusing. "Jack Sprat and his Wife," and "The House that Jack Built" being most cleverly carried out. The programme also included the infants' Quadrille, "The Cat's Duet," given by W. Trash and W Livingstone, the song "Come Back to Erin" by M Clark, and a sketch, "Apartments to Let." played by E. Smith, "Romes Stiggins, Esq."; J. Trash, "Larry Doolan"; W. Walsh, "Benjamin Bowbell"; J. Berry, "Schnider Sourkrout." During the interval the Rev. E. Marsh spoke a few words of thanks to the teachers and the children who had arranged the entertainment, also to the audience for patronising it. He also pointed out that those present were not only giving themselves pleasure, but were helping to give him the means to carry on the work of the Salesian Orphanage, on whose behalf the entertainment was arranged.

~~~

The Salesian Sisters

St. Maria Mazzarello

The Apostolate of the Salesian Sisters came to Farnborough from Battersea in 1905, their duties being to take care of the domestic arrangements at the orphanage. The Sisters are members of the congregation of the Daughters of Mary Help of Christians, FMA (Figlie Maria Ausilietrice) who were founded in 1872 by St. Maria Mazzarello, in collaboration with St. John Bosco, for the salvation of young girls.

Maria was borne on the 9th. May 1837 at Mornese, Northern Italy. Thirty five years later, she became the first Superior General of the congregation. Maria will always be remembered for her dedication, joy and love of the young.

From 1927 onwards, the Salesian Sisters were to play an important part in the teaching profession at St. Patrick's School.

*****

The Death of Father Riordan

Father Riordan

It had been evident for some years that Fr. Riordan had been losing his grip on things: he had experienced a very bad breakdown in health and it was clear that his work in Aldershot must soon come to an end. The Bishop made his visitation on 16th. December 1901, and Fr. Riordan agreed to resign as soon as a successor could be appointed. However his actual resignation did not take final effect until February 1902.

On May 29th, the Feast of Corpus Christi, he fell seriously ill. The doctor informed the clergy that when he was called for the first time "Fr. Riordan appeared to be someone who had spent his strength for other people." He died on the 31st May 1902, aged 56. The news came as a sad blow. He had worked in the town of Aldershot for 18 years. The congregation loved him with sincerity.

Fr. Riordan had almost reached the thirtieth year of his sacerdotal life and the news of his death was received with sincere regret leaving Catholic people in the town in mourning. His loss was felt by all classes; he was a man of many virtues, the most prominent being his love for the poor.

He was born in Woolwich on the 7th December 1845, and after his preliminary education had been completed he was sent to St. Edmunds College, Ware. He then went on to complete his theological studies at Hammersmith.

Ordained in 1873, by Cardinal Manning, he served as assistant priest for seven years at Mellior Street, Bermondsey, and for three years at Guernsey in the Channel Islands and was afterwards engaged as Acting Chaplain to the troops at Portsmouth. Subsequently, in 1884, he moved to Aldershot: taking up his duties as Rector of St Joseph's where he devoted the most valuable years of his life to the churches and surrounding schools. He also served on the Aldershot School Board and the Farnham Board of Guardians. Most notably, he was the founder member of St. Patrick's School.

The Lamp, a catholic periodical magazine of 1894, stated the following from Father Edward Riordan's Biography.

'Father Riordan is nothing if not a worker, he cannot be idle. How he attends to everything, considering the extent of his parish, and having no assistant, is beyond our comprehension. However, in conclusion, we may say he is every inch a true pastor of God's Church, and we hope he may be spared for many years to continue the good work he is doing, not for any reward in this world, but for that eternal reward which is to come, when our Lord will say to him, "Well done thou good and faithful servant."

Father Riordan was buried on the 5th. June 1902 at Redan Road cemetery, Aldershot.
In memory to him and his devotion to the church and catholic schools, the local parishioners raised funds and placed a crucifix of white marble at his grave with an inscription in Latin which, when translated, reads: "Jesus Christ, yesterday, to-day and the same for ever." Edward Riordan, for 18 years Rector of St. Joseph's church, passed away in the embrace of Our Lord on the last day of May, 1902. "Likened to the Son of God, a priest for ever."

*****

The Following Years

In September 1903 Farnborough Urban District Council reported that four elementary schools in Farnborough were experiencing overcrowding in both the mixed and infant departments. They were: St. Patrick's, St. Mark's, the Wesleyan's in South Farnborough, and the National school in North Farnborough.

The Council concluded: It will be seen that the accommodation of all the schools without exception is overtaxed, and that provision of additional school buildings will soon become a pressing necessity.

Paving the Way

In July 1907 the school sent an application to the Education Department to enlarge the main schoolroom. However, they were unsuccessful on this occasion.

A second application to increase the school accommodation to one hundred and forty two was approved by the Board of Education in February 1910. This was done by the rearrangement of the classrooms within the school thus improving the infant capacity to thirty seven and the mixed classes to one hundred and five. The average attendance at this time was one hundred and sixteen. In the meantime, the school had employed an extra teacher to cope with the number of pupils and, by February 1911, there were four teachers employed at the school.

~~~

A New College

The Salesian Fathers had in mind ideas to create a new collegiate school. However, they were unable to raise sufficient funds for the project to go ahead. To address the issue they decided to transfer the orphans to other neighbouring orphanages within the diocese. Their plan was endorsed and, by October 1907, the Fathers had converted the premises of the orphanage into a private school for boys: The Salesian College, South Farnborough.

~~~

From 1907 the Catholic Committee organised a series of socials which were held at the Town Hall in Reading Road, South Farnborough, the most popular of these being the annual St. Patrick's night gathering, the first of which took place in March 1908 when over 300 people attended a grand Irish night, as reported by the *Aldershot News*:

CATHOLIC SOCIAL

The sixth of the series of Catholic socials held in the Town Hall on Tuesday evening, took the form of a grand Irish night, and was specially enjoyable; indeed, it will be no exaggeration to say that it was one of the most successful of the series. There were over 300 present, and a delightful time was spent from seven o'clock until one o'clock on Wednesday morning in alternate music and dancing.

~~~

In order to raise funds for school treats, concerts were organised by the school committee in which the children performed various operettas, their costumes having been partly made at the Salesian Tailor's shop. The most prominent of these concerts was a juvenile operetta performed on the 17th December 1909, as reported by the *Aldershot News:*

JUVERNILE OPERETTA

Considering the very wintry weather which prevailed on Wednesday evening, there was a very good attendance in the Town Hall to see the performance by the children of the Catholic Elementary School of the Juvenile Operetta, "Snow White and the Seven Dwarfs." The proceeds will be given to the fund for providing the children with a Christmas treat. The children performed their parts very creditably and in a manner that reflected the highest possible praise on Miss Crowley and Miss Wilkins.

~~~

Childhood Memories of James Hunt

James Hunt must have been one of the school's most successful students both academically and in sport as well. A gifted child, here he gives us all a glimpse of his achievements, both at St. Patrick's and the Salesian College:

'I was born in 1906, and in 1911, at the tender age of five years, I commenced my education at St Patrick's Catholic School in Peabody Road. The headmistress was Miss Crowley and Miss Parish took care of the infants department.

'Although my home was very near St Patrick's School, I was invariably late in arriving at school in the mornings in spite of the threats of punishment or promise of reward. Finally, Miss Crowley had a brilliant idea. She created for me the post of "MONITOR OF THE SCHOOL CLOCK" with a scenario ideally suited to a couple of comedians.

'The clock was high on the wall and, initially, it was necessary to locate the step ladder. Once in place, I mounted to the top, and from this position it was possible to see through the window a large clock in the distance, and from this, at exactly 9 o'clock, I adjusted the school clock.

'Every morning, for a few minutes, all attention was focused on me! As I mounted the steps in hushed silence, half the children hoping I would fall and break my neck and the less blood thirsty ones hoping I would get the time wrong. In any case, Miss Crowley had won, and I was never late again. I would not risk losing my star billing roll!

'Having passed my Scholarship at St. Patrick's towards the end of 1918, I then began some of the happiest days of my life when I became a student at the Salesian College, Farnborough. My age was just twelve and I was allotted to form 1VB, to be taught by Brother Gerald and Mr. Shorney. At that time the school had about 200 pupils, of which about 160 – 170 were boarders, as far as I can recollect, and about 20 – 30 were day boys. In addition, there were always 10 – 20 foreign students who stayed perhaps a year, sometimes more, for a purpose of practising their English language orally. Many came from South America, Argentina, Venezuela etcetera.

'Those pupils at the school who loved sport, as I did, had a great time. Every free minute was filled with football, cricket, tennis according to the season, and the masters joined in always. The first elevens played the local senior and army teams of varying strength. We also went away to play Battersea, Wandsworth, and other Salesian Colleges.

'1923 was my last year as a pupil, and a most successful year for me it proved. I was the only one to pass London Metrication examination. I also passed Oxford Senior Certificate exam with honours and two distinctions, and about six weeks later I passed College of Preceptors Senior Examination. The preparation for this exam, in such a short time following the Oxford Senior exams, was very difficult. All the set books were different of course. Anyway, the results were worth it, and my photo made the "Honour Cui Honour" page in the January 1924 edition of the School Magazine

'As regards sport, I played in the first eleven for both football and cricket and set school records for the half mile and quarter mile. A most satisfying year.'

James sent in an application to teach at St. Mary's Catholic Training College and, while waiting for the decision, taught forms IVB and II and was accepted at St. Mary's. Sadly, he was unable to take up the position because his parents could not afford the cost of the fees and books, there being no grants in those far off days. However, he continued teaching in Farnborough for eighteen months. He then became a private tutor to a family of retired tea-planters who lived in Church Crookham after which he took up a long-lasting career in the Insurance industry, eventually retiring at the age of 61.

~~~

Organised Treats

Mr. and Mrs Wilkes, who lived at Arnold House in Alexander Road, South Farnborough, would occasionally organise treats for St. Patrick's school children. Mr. Wilkes, who served on the Farnborough and District Council, also had a desire to see Farnborough grow and prosper, while Mrs. Wilkes was a social worker and was particularly interested in the welfare of children. Together they gave help and support to the benefit of the Borough. So it was a pleasant surprise for St. Patrick's school when the happy and generous couple sent an invitation inviting the whole school to attend Mrs. Wilkes's birthday party to partake of 'tea, as reported by the *Sheldrakes Military Gazette on 15th September 1911:*

King's Message to School Children

On Saturday last Mrs. Wilkes, of Arnold House, celebrated her birthday, and in a most kindly manner entertained the whole of the children of Peabody Road Catholic Schools to tea on the lawn of her residence, and subsequently to a most happy hour's entertainment. Those of the scholars with the best school records received a souvenir in the form of a Coronation mug. The kindness of the lady was hugely appreciated by the happy youngsters.

During the progress of the entertainment the following message was sent to H. M. the King, at Balmoral.

"One hundred and nine loyal little subjects of the Farnborough Roman Catholic Schools, now having tea at Arnold House, send their humble duty to the King, and wish him long life and good health."

In a short space of time the following reply was received from His Majesty:

"The King thanks his little subjects from the Roman Catholic Schools for their loyalty and good wishes."

It should be added that the children, who also gave an entertainment themselves, presented their kind hostess with a beautiful bouquet, which they had subscribed to, and which was greatly appreciated. Before leaving each had a helping of the birthday cake and were sent away home possessors of a full bag of sweets.

The following year in January 1912, Mr. and Mrs Wilkes once more showed their generosity, organising treats for the school, as reported by the *Aldershot News*:

HAPPY SCHOOL CHILDREN

MR AND MRS WILKES' GENEROSITY

It is with much pleasure we record the happy scenes that took place in the Catholic Elementary Schools, Farnborough, last week when through the unfailing kindness of Mr. and Mrs. Wilkes of Arnold House, the children had a most enjoyable entertainment at the new Electric Theatre in Camp Road, and a most sumptuous tea and Christmas Tree in the evening.

Last summer Mr. and Mrs. Wilkes promised two medals to the scholars of the school, one in the senior and the other in the infant's department, for the best attendance and general good conduct, with the result that it was found most difficult to select the candidates, on account of the excellent way in which the children strove to win the coveted prizes. This energy on the part of the children was naturally a great consolation to their teachers, and it must have helped, in no small way to obtain the high encomiums of H. M. Inspector, namely, that he had nothing but praise for the efficiency of the school.

It was during an interval in the performance at the theatre that the medals won, were presented to Richard Pavill and George Duffield, while a special prize went to Eileen Cousins, and a fitted-up writing-desk went to Paul Dunham. Mr. Wilkes, in an admirable speech which created loud applause took the occasion to congratulate the happy children on their splendid record and said what a pleasure it was to him and Mrs. Wilkes to show their appreciations of such good conduct.

Father Sutherland, Rector of the mission on behalf of the teachers and children, thanked Mr. and Mrs. Wilkes for their great kindness, and continuing, he said the people of Farnborough all appreciated the great charity of Mr. and Mrs. Wilkes, and knew that their principal object in life, was to make others happy especially poor children, and surely it must be a real joy to them that day, to know that they had shed so much happiness into the lives of so many little ones.

After the performance at the theatre, the children returned to the school, where they found their cosy classrooms beautifully decorated with festoons and garlands of flowers. The scene before the children was indeed entrancing. Mr. Wilkes, with excellent taste and willing helpers, had spent the whole morning and the previous afternoon in decorating the school. The tables were heavily laden with all kinds of delicacies, cakes, sweets, fruit, bon-bons, etc. etc. and the happy children showed by their merry faces that their lot was indeed a happy one.

Next came a real live Father Christmas in the person of Miss Cooper, niece of Mr. and Mrs. Wilkes, who after having donned the costume suitable to the occasion, caused great merriment when distributing in her mysterious way, a gift to everyone present.

Among those who assisted were the teachers, Miss Crowley (head mistress), Miss Warmington, Miss Kerens, Miss Parish, and among the visitors were the Very Rev. Father Sutherland, and the Rev. Fathers, Gittinan and Norman. S.C., Mrs. Pinckney, Miss Wilkins, Mr and Mrs Dallenger, Mrs Parsons, Mrs Skivier and Mr Wakely, etc.

At nine o'clock, the party broke up after a most enjoyable evening, amidst great cheering for Mr. and Mrs. Wilkes.

~~~

In October 1912 an outing had been arranged for the Catholic Schools to visit the Picture House. A first class tea was then enjoyed followed by prizes donated on behalf of Mr. and Mrs. Wilkes, as reported by Sheldrakes Military Gazette:

Children's Happy Treat

Thanks to the extreme kindness of Mr. and Mrs. Wilkes, of Arnold House, some 120 children of the Catholic day schools have just been accorded a most happy entertainment. Under the charge of their mistress, Miss Crowley, and staff, with their entertainers, fully this number were made free of the picture palace, and heartily enjoyed a special programme that had been arranged for their benefit, and at the conclusion they returned to the schools, where they were regaled with a first class tea, and to which they did the best of justice.

The Very Rev. Father Sutherland was unable to be present, but was represented by the Rev. Giltinan, who referred in terms of warm appreciation of the great kindness of Mr. and Mrs. Wilkes, and to the interest which they had always taken in the school. Mrs. Wilkes made a practice of offering a prize for the best needlework amongst the girls in the upper divisions, and also a prize for reading in the infants' department, and these prizes were awarded, for needlework to Eileen Cussens first, and Sybil Jennings second; and to the infants, Mary Jane Pryce, first; and James Hunt, second. A watch offered to the boy making the best attendance and best behaviour by the Very Rev. Father Sutherland was won by Master Hugh Weston, and the prize was presented to him on behalf of the donor by the Rev. Father Giltinan. It need scarcely be added that the children accorded the heartiest of cheers to Mr. and Mrs. Wilkes and to their governess and staff for all they had done, not excluding Mrs. Scivor, who rendered valued assistance with the tea.

~~~

In September 1913 an interesting and diverse outing was arranged for the Catholic Schools to visit Compton near Godalming, Surrey, as reported by Sheldrakes Military Gazette:

School Children's Outing

On Saturday the children attending the Catholic elementary schools were made very happy in that they were taken by brakes to Compton. They were accompanied by the Rev. T. J. Giltinan, S.C., of the Salesian staff, and were regaled with a first class tea, all kinds of outdoor sports following. The visit to this charming rendezvous, as well as the long drive out, and the return journey, helped to make one of the most enjoyable events in the children's holiday. It should be added that the treat was secured to the children by the kindness of the Rev. A. Sutherland. Amongst those who rendered great help, together with Miss Crowley, headmistress, were Mr. and Mrs. G. Davis, Messrs' H. Gillman and G. Walsh.

*****

The First World War and Beyond

The Catholic and Salesian committee's continued to organize fund raising socials up to the beginning of the First World War after which time they were discontinued. Unfortunately, little information exists on the school's activities during the First World War. However, between 1914 and 1918, garden fetes were still being organized and took place at the Park Road playing fields, which the Salesian's had previously purchased from the Farnborough Games Club in 1911.

The school organised outings over the Christmas periods to the Empire Electric Theatre in Lynchford Road. Mr. and Mrs Wilkes together with the support of the Salesian Father's and their teaching staff then followed these up with seasonal parties.

As a result of teachers and children saving during this period, a donation was made from the school of £9-0s-6d to the Farnborough Court Auxiliary Hospital. The Hospital was run by the British Red Cross for wounded service men and was situated near to Farnborough Monastery.

In November 1917 His Majesty's Inspector reported to the local Education Authorities that a number of truancies existed in their local schools, St Marks, St. Patrick's and Queen's Road, and that the attendance officer was discharging his duties in an unsatisfactory way. He also quoted in his report: *It is creditable to the several head teachers concerned that the general state of attendance is not much less satisfactory than it is.*

The average school attendance at St. Patrick's during this period is as follows: 1916 – one hundred and fifteen; 1917 – one hundred and seven and in 1918 – one hundred and eight.

~~~

Memories of Reginald Hunt

Reginald, younger brother of James Hunt, grew up in Peabody Road and attended St. Patrick's in 1920. Aged 97, he now lives in Selsey on the Sussex coast. When I spoke to him, he told me that the toilets were located at the front of the school in a square block and had no roof. He also mentioned that the playground to the rear of the school was just dirt and stones and was separated from a field by bushes and trees, which backed on to Sherborne Road.

I also found out that he was a keen sportsman, because he heartily told me that he played both cricket and football for the school team.

'I remember when we were playing football, we wore black and green shirts and black shorts.' he said. 'And some of the teams we played against were: St. Mark's, and Queens Road in Farnborough, Yorktown, Camberley, and also Sandhurst. Of course, when we played Queens Road it was a local derby match, and on one occasion we lost 23 goals to 2!' 'However,' he proudly went on to say, 'I scored the two goals for St Patrick's.'

Reginald also remembers receiving his first Holy Communion in 1923, at Our Lady Help of Christians church. This was followed by the annual Corpus Christi Procession in the Salesian College Grounds after which we had our photos taken with Fr. Hawarden and the teachers.

Teachers he remembers were: Miss Alice Crowley, 'the Governess – who was very prim and proper', Miss Mary Parish and Sister Frances.

~~~

First Communion 1923: Top left: Miss Alice Crowley. Top right: teacher unknown.
Fr. Hawarden is in the centre. Reginald Hunt is in the front row bottom left and his cousin Ronald Ivil is second left in the middle row. All other communicants are unknown.

~~~

Staff and Management Committee

In 1922, Drew's Directory for Aldershot, Farnborough and District quoted the following staff and Management committee at St. Patrick's School:

Staff: Miss Alice Crowley (Headmistress), Miss Mary Parish, Miss O'Leary and Miss Miller.

Committee of Management: Rev. M. H. McCarthy (Chairman and Correspondent), Rev. J. F. McCourt, Rev. P. Williams and Mr G. W. Collins, J.P., C.C.

~~~

Memories of Mary Rush (nee Hunt)

Mary Rush, sister of Reginald Hunt, started at St. Patrick's in 1926 and has fond memories of taking part in athletics and playing netball for the school. Mary recalled that they played in green and yellow and that they won some and lost some!

She received her First Holy Communion in 1928, which, she remembered, was a special occasion held jointly with the May Day celebrations. The procession was held in the Salesian grounds in honour of Our Lady for which the month of May is traditionally dedicated by Catholics.

Teachers Mary remembers during her time: Miss Alice Crowley, Miss Mary Parish, Miss Gladys Hoyes and Sister Frances Pedrick.

May Day and First Holy Communion with Fr. Giltinan in 1928: Left to right:
Rosie Lester, unknown, Ron Waite, Doreen Palmer, Doris Caiger, Marcelle Fonteneau,
Mary Rush and ? Newman.

May Day statue bearers of Our Lady, 1935. Left to right: Winnie Sheehan, Mary Hunt,
Mary Moore and Eileen Nobble.

*****

Alice Crowley's Retirement ~ School children's farewell

Alice Crowley

Tuesday 28th May 1927 was to bring both joy and sadness to all those present on the day of Alice Crowley's retirement. Miss Crowley started teaching at Farnborough in February 1893 where she was given the honour of officially opening the school under the Board of Education Act.

During his speech at the presentation Father Sutherland referred to Miss Crowley as a great builder of character whose constant care and solicitude for her pupils was a credit to the school. Miss Crowley has been an ideal type of teacher. She has been most conscientious in her duties and most fair to those under her charge. The *Aldershot News* gave an interesting report of the ceremony during her final day at the school. The following of which mentions:

PRESENTATION TO HEAD TEACHER

There were sad and joyous scenes in the Peabody Road School on Tuesday week, when Miss Alice Crowley severed her official connection with the school of which she had been headmistress for 34 years. The many gifts presented to her showed the great esteem in which she is held by teachers and scholars alike. The school was prettily decorated for the occasion, and among those present were the Rev. A. Sutherland, Rev. A. Hawarden and Rev. J. A. Muldoon. Mary Hunt presented a bouquet of pink and white carnations to Miss Crowley, and then the senior boy, Robert Creighton, read a letter of farewell from the children and teachers, and on their behalf Kathleen Grenham presented to Miss Crowley a black morocco handbag. Robert Ivil presented to her a framed photograph of the scholars and teachers and Eileen Haggart presented Miss Crowley with an album containing the signatures of all the children attending the school. Other children presented Miss Crowley with their own individual gifts.

Short speeches by the Rev. A. Sutherland, A. Hawarden and J. Muldoon preceded a brief and touching response from Miss Crowley. The ceremony concluded with ringing cheers for the "head" and the singing of "For she's a jolly good teacher." When Miss Crowley left the school in a taxicab the children followed to her home in York Road, and remained outside for some time, cheering lustily.

*****

Pro Ecclesia et Pontifice

Recognition by the Pope

On the evening of Tuesday the 19th. June 1927, the Town Hall was filled with Catholics from Farnborough, Aldershot and the surrounding areas to witness the investiture of the Cross, "Pro Ecclesia et Pontifice" (For God and for the Church.) on Miss Alice Crowley who was rewarded for her service in recognition of a long and distinguished career at St. Patrick's School when the decoration of The Cross was bestowed upon her by His Holiness Pope Pius XI. The ceremony was performed by Monsignor John Maloney V.G., OBE. MC., SCF., with the Pope's blessing, which read, *"May it be a pledge of the great honour and glory you will get in the Kingdom to come."* Having received her medal Miss Crowley was then given a great ovation by a large crowd consisting of pupils, former pupils, teachers and parishioners.

A report by the diocesan inspector Rev. Fr. Dorran, referring to the loyal and devoted work of Miss Crowley, stated … *"that the religious work at the school was always eminently satisfactory and last years' work was no exception to the general rule."*

The Rev. Edward Muldoon S.C., representing the Friends and Parishioners of Catholic Farnborough then expressed *"admiration, respect and deep gratitude for Miss Crowley's brilliant work in the interests of their elementary schools over such a long span of years."* He also referred to Miss Crowley as *"An accomplished Head Mistress, a perfect lady, an inspiring teacher and the children's friend."*

Mr. W.W. Miller, representing the teachers of the Elementary schools in Farnborough, congratulated Miss Crowley on the great honour conferred upon her by the Pope and said: *He wished to record the teacher's appreciation of Miss Crowley's work for the education of Farnborough children.* He also said, *In spite of all the modern education authorities, Miss Crowley had retained her keenness and enthusiasm for her scholastic duties and had kept pace with the times which, he assured them, was very difficult to do.*

Miss Crowley was loudly cheered and replied by thanking everyone present for their allegiance. She also thanked Fr. Sutherland for his untiring labours in obtaining for her the High Honour of the Decoration of the Cross, which she would always treasure more than anything else

Speaking of her pride in serving at St. Patrick's, she expressed further thanks for the many gifts that she had received, which included a magnificent silver tea service, wristlet watch, and a framed address and letter eulogising her services during the 34 years as head mistress of the school.

Finally, Miss Crowley paid tribute to the school children for appearing in such numbers and the teachers of whom she said had worked ardently and well; they could not have done any more. She also wished to proclaim her gratitude to the pope for granting Fr. Sutherland's request.

The award is known as the "Cross of Honour" and was established by Pope Leo XIII in 1888 to commemorate His Priestly Jubilee. It was awarded to lay persons and clergy for distinguished service to the church. At the time, it was also bestowed upon women, too. However, in more recent times, women have been awarded the Order of St. Gregory.

*****

A New Dawn

Sister Frances Marie Rose Pedrick FMA MA

Sister Frances Pedrick took over as Headmistress from Alice Crowley in 1927; perhaps a daunting task after Miss Crowley's magnificent success. The following notes are from the *Salesian Sisters' Archives, Liverpool.*

Born on the 19th. November 1887 into a big-hearted, numerous family with parents that were strongly Christian, she was surrounded by a love that she was to transmit to others later on. She was baptised on the 4th. December1887, and confirmed on the 19th September 1897 in Teignmouth, Devon. Each member of her family could sing and play an instrument and so music, which was to be an integral part of her later life, was fostered and enjoyed in her home.

Frances owed a lot to the Sisters of Notre Dame, in whose convent she became a border. Of the Head Mistress, Frances said "I owe her an eternal debt of gratitude. If I am what I am today it is through her great kindness and unselfish generosity." Frances became a pupil teacher in the Notre Dame School. She began to feel the call of God and confided to her Parish Priest that she felt she had a vocation for the religious life. Her Parish Priest told her of Don Bosco and his method of education based on the love of God and of the child. He spoke to her of St. Mary Mazzarello and the Daughters of Mary Help of Christians who were doing for girls what Don Bosco was doing for boys. This priest, knowing the magnetic influence Frances had with young people, knowing too, how she loved little children and how they loved her, advised her to write to the Salesian Sisters in Chertsey. She did so and entered the convent in Chertsey in 1911. The Convent was poor, the work hard but Frances, with her joyful enthusiasm, made little of the sacrifices.

Professed in 1913 she was put to study and gained her teacher's certificate and then an honours degree at Oxford University. Even while studying she still found time to run an Oratory where the girls used to flock around her. She taught first at a small private school at our convent in Cowley and then on to Farnborough where she was Head Mistress of a mixed school of boys and girls: St. Patrick's.

~~~

A Creditable Account

The following school report for May 1928 gave a creditable account of Sister Frances and her staff as reported by His Majesty's Inspector:

The last report indicated that the work of this school was on the whole satisfactory. It is now possible to go a little further and say that a steady advance on the previous position has been made that the future prospects of the school are most encouraging. In History & Geography, where some grounds for adverse criticism existed, distinct improvement is noticeable.

The present Headmistress, who has been in charge rather less than a year, devotes herself unselfishly to the welfare of the school. She is well supported by her staff, whose hard work deserves full recognition.

Premises The condition of the playground is extremely unsatisfactory. The loose stones should be removed & a smooth surface provided.

~~~

Come and Live Longer at Farnborough

In order to attract people into the town, John Drew, a local printer, in collaboration with the Urban District Council and the Chamber of Commerce, published a book in 1929 called "Come and Live Longer at Farnborough." The following can be found under the heading of Elementary Schools:

St. Patrick's Elementary Day School, Peabody-road: Headmistress, Sister Frances Pedrick, F.M.A., M.A. (Oxon). Committee of Management: Very Rev. M. H. McCarthy. Chairman: Rev. T. J. Giltinan. Correspondents: Rev P. Williams, Rev E Muldoon, Mr W. L. McIntyre D. C. M. and Mrs. Frankham.

~~~

The Knights of St. Columba

The Knights of St. Columba is an Order of Catholic Laymen dedicated to the service of the church and fellow men that conforms to the principles of charity, unity and fraternity in the Catholic Church. The Order was founded in 1919 by Patrick O'Callaghan and named after St. Columba, a Christian missionary who helped to spread Christianity to Scotland in the 6th century.

And, so it was, that charity flourished on a Friday in July 1930 when the Knights presented a House Challenge Shield to the school on its second, Annual Sports Day.

St Patrick's Second Annual Sports Day

On this special and exciting day, the events took place on the spacious Salesian playing fields in Park Road and were most remarkable in their diversity of events for boys and girls of all ages as listed below:-

80, 100, 120, and 220 yards races; high jump, long jump and half mile handicap; skipping, and throwing the stool ball; relay races, sack races and arithmetic races!; hurdles, obstacle races and throwing the cricket ball. And last, but not least, potato races!

As we can all imagine, it was a fully fun-packed day for parents and competitors alike. Those gaining the highest amount of points were awarded medals in both the junior and senior sections for both boys and girls.

At the end of the day, St Francis of Assisi House gained 60 points, and lifted the shield, while St. Clare House finished a close second with 57 points.

The children had been trained by the deputy head, Miss Gladys Hoyes, who came to the school in 1928.

The Knights continued their support for St. Patrick's, organising socials and helping to raise funds for the school up until 1939. By then, the Catholic Women's League had also become involved.

~~~

A New Classroom

By 1932 conditions in the classrooms had become cramped. However, in February His Majesty's Inspector reported: *'This school is doing good work under rather crowded and difficult conditions. The HT and her assistants are working with great earnestness & devotion to duty. The spirit and behaviour of the children are excellent.'*

The New Classroom

In April the school committee made an application to the Board of Education for the building of a new classroom which would be sited to the rear of the main building. The application was accepted in November and the classroom was completed and ready for use in 1934. The school now had four classrooms with a capacity for 183 pupils. The new classroom had a capacity for fifty children and was also used as a Youth Club facility. During this time the playground was extended as far as Sherborne Road, the land having been previously purchased by the Salesian Fathers.

Improvements to the school took place in August 1936 when electric lighting and central heating was installed. New lavatories were also erected at each side of the playground at a cost of almost £800, and were paid for out of school funds. The playground was also surfaced. Further improvements were carried out in 1938 when new offices were erected for the staff.

~~~

Memories of Renee Newcombe (nee Tottle)

Renee Newcombe, whose father owned Tottle's Newsagent's shop in Peabody Road, started at St. Patrick's in 1931. Renee has fond memories of the May Day processions which were held in the Salesian College courtyard. "In 1935 my sister, Rosemary, was chosen May Queen and had the honour of crowning the statue of Our Lady. And we both received our First Communion in Our Lady Help of Christians Church, Queens Road" she said. "I also remember the annual ceremony was held in June and was followed by the Corpus Christi Procession.

"Though I had the opportunity to go to the Hillside Convent, I chose to go to the County High School in Aldershot. Having reached my teens, I became a member of the Children of Mary which was organised by the Salesian Sisters. When attending we wore a blue cloak and a white veil" she said.

Teachers that she remembers were Sister Francis Pedrick, Miss Mary Parish and Miss Gladys Hoyes. 'All of the teachers were nice. However, I admired Miss Hoyes most of all.'

First Holy Communion 1933.

Middle row, fifth from left: Renee Tottle. The other communicants are unknown.

First Holy Communion 1935, with Fr. Cressey.

Front row, third left: Rosemary Tottle. The other communicants are unknown.

May Day 1935: Rosemary Tottle is at the front of the crowning ceremony.

~~~

Mary Parish's Retirement

The following report from the *Catholic Herald* on the 1st. July 1938 gave a credible account to Mary Parish on the occasion of her retirement.

A TEACHER's RECORD - NO ADVERSE REPORT OVER 43 YEARS

At the conclusion of the evening service at the church of Our Lady Help of Christians, Farnborough, on Sunday last, the parishioners assembled in large numbers upon the lawn of the Salesian College to do honour to Miss Mary Parish, who has just retired after 43 years of devoted service in St Patrick's Elementary School.

At the gathering, presided over by Mr. George Davis, one of the oldest parishioners, Fr. Sutherland, S.C. (rector) was able to present Miss Parish, on behalf of the many subscribers, with a cheque for over £60. The Pope sent his Apostolic Benediction, whilst the Bishop of Portsmouth and the Rev. F. Dorran (Diocesan Religious Inspector) wrote in glowing terms of a wonderful work Miss Parish had done. It is a singular fact that during the 43 years of her service – easily a local record – she had never received an adverse report from any of H.M. Inspectors.

At a presentation earlier in the week the children of the elementary school presented Miss Parish with a gold watch as a sign of their affection.

~~~

Sister Frances Pedrick's Retirement

Sister Frances

Sister Frances retired in September 1938 after eleven years' service. During her time at the school Sister Frances was mostly involved with teaching the senior pupils. Her main subject was music and she could often be heard playing the piano, while the senior class were singing English folk songs.

She also organised outings to the convent at Chertsey for children who had passed their scholarships and helped the children prepare for the May Day and Corpus Christi events.

Her other interest was the involvement in the supervision of the Children of Mary, a community of teenage girls who were sworn to Sodality, based on the principles of purity, humility, obedience and charity, the latter being involved in arranging events for the local Catholic Churches.

Former pupil, Reginald Hunt, remembered her playing the piano and referred to Sister Frances as a 'Darling lady.' An extract from a letter written by a past pupil of St. Patrick's, shows just how much Sister Frances was revered by those children:

"When I left school you gave me a missal. It now lies at the bottom of the English Channel as a result of an encounter with an enemy destroyer about ten miles off Cherbourg. Inside the cover you had written several reminders and advice, such as 'Remember your morning and evening prayers and your weekly confession.' Do you remember your last note? I have never forgotten it. 'Never do anything that would make you blush in front of others.' So you see, Sister, there must be hundreds of us who started our working life armed with your guidance and prayers"

Having retired from St. Patrick's, Sister Frances went on to teach at Eastwood Road Convent School at Chertsey. The school was privately owned by the Salesian Sisters who taught infant and junior pupils. However, the school closed sometime during the 1960s at which time Sister Frances retired from teaching altogether.

Sister Ann Darwin also taught at Chertsey and mentioned to me that Sister Frances was 'a gentle, warm and loving person and a terrific educator.' She also mentioned that Sister Frances was devoted to the Sacred Heart, and could often be heard saying 'Sacred Heart of Jesus, I place my trust in you. Sacred Heart of Jesus, I will always trust in you.'

Note: In 1931 Sister Frances was absent from the school due to illness from February until the following October. During this period, her position was taken by Sister Marion Watts.

*****

A Time for Change

Sister Marie came to St. Patrick's in 1938 and took over the Headship following Sister Frances Pedrick's retirement, her subjects being English and Music.

The following notes are from the Salesian Sisters' archive, Liverpool. *Marie was born in Chelsea on 2nd. May 1909, the eldest of six daughters. When Marie felt the call to religious life she spoke to the parish clergy and curate, a past pupil of the Salesian College Farnborough who pointed her in the direction of the Salesian Sisters in Battersea. She entered the convent at Chertsey on the 27th. January 1925 and was admitted as a postulant two days later on 29th. January, then the feast of St. Frances de Sales.*

She graduated in 1935 as an infant and junior teacher from the Immaculate Conception teacher training college at Southampton.

Sister Marie

The following is from Sister Marie's memoires:

"*After teaching in convent independent schools in Chertsey, Cowley, Limerick (Eire), and in a European school for children in Madras, I came back to England in April, 1938 to take up the post of Infants Teacher at St. Patricks. This was followed by appointment to the Headship in September of that same year.*

The school then consisted of four classes, taught by the Head and three assistants, in what is the main building at Peabody Road. Numbers varied between 120 and 140 pupils, and there were three lobbies, two of which had old black-iron wash basins.

"*One of the assistants left in December 1939, and the Authority would not grant a replacement, so the school divided into Infants, Juniors and Seniors. After a lot of hard pressing by the Management, we eventually got a replacement in September, 1940.*"

~~~

The Planning of a New School

In 1938 St. Joseph's Roman Catholic school, Aldershot, under the Education Act of 1923, applied for a grant to the Education Authorities to build a new Senior Secondary school catering for 160 children. The school would be sited in St. Joseph's Road, Aldershot at a cost of £9,000, excluding the cost of the ground. However, after consultations with other local schools a second proposal was put to the authorities to include Catholic children from Camberley, Farnborough, and Farnham. Consultation continued up until December when the Aldershot Education Committee consented to providing sufficient accommodation for children coming from Camberley, Farnborough and Farnham areas, albeit subject to both Hampshire and Surrey Authority's approval.

By March 1939 the Surrey and Hampshire Councils had agreed to pay for the education of the children from these areas. However, the new school would now have to cater for 240 pupils and, as a result, school managers had to submit new estimates.

Sadly, the scheme was thwarted when war broke out the following September, leaving the Board of Education having no choice but to suspend all grants.

~~~

The Irish Players

The Irish Players were an eclectic mix of dramatic society performers who came from differing backgrounds. There remit was, not only to perform plays that emanated entirely from the Emerald Isle, but also to raise funds for charitable causes.

One of the actors was Mrs. Sproule, who had performed at the Abbey Theatre, Dublin. The plays, which were performed in the 1930s, were exceedingly humorous, and were put on at the Town Hall, Farnborough, as reported by the *Aldershot News*:

FARNBOROUGH'S NEW DRAMATIC SOCIETY

An excellent cast had been assembled, with three members of the R.A.E. Dramatic Society, Mr. E. Lawlor, Mr. E. P. Ferguson and Mr. A. S. Hartshorn, playing important parts. But undoubtedly the star of the evening was Mrs. G. M. Sproule (the wife of Brevet Major G. M. M.C., R.A.S.C. Sproule) *who produced both plays, and as Eithne McGee appeared in "The Building Fund" as an old crone,* and also in *"Spreading the News", as a very attractive young married woman.*

"The Building Fund", was *a three act play about a miserly old woman hoarding every penny, and snapping and snarling at those who were waiting around for the pickings after her death,* while "Spreading the News", was a one act play that was: *"a racy skit on the Irish habit of unrestrained gossiping."*

Along with other charitable organizations that benefited from the Players excellent performances was St. Patrick's Building Fund.

~~~

The Catholic Women's League

In March 1939, St. Patrick's school hosted a meeting of the Catholic Women's League, its remit being to establish a branch of the League in Farnborough. A social event was then arranged for the following month at the school where the League was successful in recruiting new members, bringing their total to thirty six in all. From time-to-time, their members organised rummage and jumble sales and, not least, Christmas bazaars, the proceeds being donated to the school's Building Fund.

The League was founded by Margaret Fletcher in 1906, its motto being Charity, Work and Loyalty. Their main aims were: To promote educational, family and social welfare issues within the parishes and the wider community.

Their patron saint is Margaret Clitherow; a young, married woman who was condemned and crushed to death for her beliefs at York on the 25th March 1586.

*****

The Second World War

The Following notes have been taken from Sister Marie's memoirs giving an account of the war years:

"This was the war period of gas-mask fitting, air-raid drills, and when the real thing came, runs to the Anderson shelters (air raid shelters) *at the Sherborne Road end of the playground. It was laid down that two teachers had to be with the infants in their shelter, so that until September 1940, that left me to look after the other two shelters, added to which, I was supposed to walk between Sherborne and Peabody Roads looking for incendiary bombs.*

"We managed by giving the children a list of songs and hymns. The strains of "Daily Daily", "The Siegfried Line", "God bless our Pope", and "Roll out the Barrel", resounded all over the playground, and served the dual purpose of letting us know what the children were up to, and drowned the noise of gunfire.

Fortunately, although the spells in shelters were rather prolonged at times, during the daytime there was very little "overhead" trouble. The older children were very bored and did not want to use the shelters, one of which was unusable, with anything between 3 and 15 inches of water covering the floor. So when two " young sparks" were found one day sitting on top of the shelter watching a dog-fight, it was thought advisable to let the older boys and girls shelter when necessary in a safe angle of the school buildings.

There was a scare one day when a hole appeared in the playground, and the caretaker's husband was sure he could hear the ticking of a time bomb. The children were sent home for the day, and ARP officials - suspecting an AA shell - took over.

(Apparently, after investigation, it was found to be due to subsidence of a drain!)

There were no school dinners, and most of the children went home for lunch. A few children from Ash Vale brought sandwiches, and it was one of my jobs to make them drinks of hot cocoa. Later I was able to employ a helper to do this.

It is remarkable, looking through the records, to find out how active and alive the school was during this period of the war. H.M. Inspectors and P.E. Advisers paid us frequent visits; scholarship examinations to grammar schools, homecraft and commercial schools, were taken with reasonable success. A conjurer paid an annual visit; we visited the Town Hall and the local cinema for exhibitions and films connected with war effort and took part in all the Weeks, during the three for "Salute the Soldier", "Wings for Victory", and "War Weapons", our salvage during each of the campaigns reached well over £100.

A letter from Sister Marie to the Education Authority dated 15th. November 1940 gave some cause for concern:

One of the air raid shelters is absolutely unusable as it is under water to a depth of about 12 inches. The boys pumped out the water yesterday but after an hour it was up again. The water seems to pour in from under the bottom step. Probably a spring has been tapped. I should be grateful if something could be done as quickly as possible because the other two shelters cannot accommodate 130 children ranging from 5 to 14 years and we have had alert signals almost every day this week. The other two shelters are also very damp as the water trickles through the joints.

The letter went on to discuss blackout arrangements, the adjustment of school times, the difficulties of children who come from distant areas and the problems encountered by the caretaker to properly clean the school.

~~~

In December 1941 Sister Marie again wrote to the Hampshire Education Authorities expressing her concern for the need for midday meals to be provided at the school:

There is no accommodation at all for a kitchen in the school building and no hut which might be adapted.

Should you find it possible to erect a centre in the vicinity of the school, however, 67 children have given their names as desirous of using it under the described conditions.

~~~

While the war raged on, three, long years were to pass by. However, in March 1944 a County Education Officer came to inspect and report on the school premises:

Farnborough R.C. School. <u>Mid-day meals.</u>

109 on books, meals required for some 80 children.
Proposed to erect a Ministry of Works kitchen on part of the playground which is not tar-paved: to cut an entrance into the classroom and to feed in the classroom.
County Architect to prepare plan.

For reasons not known the school management decided to decline the offer and two more years passed by without a positive decision being made. Eventually, Sister Marie decided to use the facilities at Queens Road School, South Farnborough.

~~~

The Passage of the Education Bill

Though a National Education Committee existed in 1944, apparently Farnborough did not have one at this time. That meant there was no expression of views from the local people in the various branches of education. The outcome was that an Advisory Committee was formed, which included heads, teachers and various organisations who were interested in education. Once it was formed, some of the proposals put forward by the Farnborough Education Committee related to school buildings were varied and diverse:

School Buildings, Etc. - *Each school, however small, should be provided with a free room or hall for the use of the children for assembly, physical training, dancing, etc. This should in no case be smaller than seven hundred sq. ft. It is suggested that the same room would possibly be used for serving school meals. Every school should be provided with covered ways to lavatories. Since in most of the old style schools, lavatories are built across the playground from the school, the hardship to little children in winter is considerable. It is felt that priority should be given to this suggestion. Playground shelters should also be provided.*

It is considered that early training in the appreciation of beautiful surroundings is as important in earlier years as later. The interior decorations should be cheerful and light in colour. The new secondary and senior schools all have pleasantly laid out gardens and lawns. The bare ugly playgrounds at present in existence should have some part at least in use as a garden cared for by the authority, apart from such gardens as are tended by the children. Since purposeful activity should be the basis of all work in primary schools furniture provided should be strong, but light in character, and easily moved by the children. Apparatus for outdoor and indoor physical exercise should be as plentifully provided as in the secondary schools. Shoes suitable for dancing, etc. should be supplied and such floors as are faulty should be re-covered.

Ventilation and heating should be brought up to date in existing schools and there should be some supply of hot water in each building.

The following recommendations were put forward for school meals:

School Meals. - *Unless the L.E.A. are in a position to provide a qualified catering staff for any given school, it is strongly recommended that a central kitchen should be organised for the cooking of school dinners for the whole area. A supervisor fully qualified in the planning of diets for children and in catering should be in charge of this. The schools should be equipped with hot-plates, serving, washing up and dining room facilities only, and the meals should be delivered to each school readily prepared. The present arrangement by which head teachers, sometimes in charge of a class, are made responsible for the catering and storekeeping is considered to be most unsatisfactory and detrimental to the welfare of the schools.*

The supervision of the meals must be undertaken by those skilled in the handling of children. At the same time, it is placing too heavy a burden on the teachers of large classes to continue throughout the day with little or no break at mid-day. It is therefore suggested that when the staffing situation is eased, part-time paid assistants might be found amongst married ex-teachers for this supervision.

Schools containing seven classes or more should be supplied with special dining room accommodation. In smaller schools a hall could serve the double purpose.

~~~

Memories of Audrey King (nee Dixon)

Audrey King started at St. Patrick's in 1940 aged five. Like all of us do, from time to time, she fondly reminisced about how things were in those difficult days:

'St. Patrick's made no provision for hot food at lunch time', she said. 'However, some of our pupils used to visit St. Martin's iron church (which was adjacent to St. Mark's School, Queens Road) where they served hot dinners to children from all the schools in the area.

'P.E. lessons were held in the school playground and our annual sports day took place on the Army Polo Fields whereas the swimming took place at the Army Command baths.'

During the war, Audrey remembered the first time she entered into one of the air raid shelters. 'Inside were two long benches, one each side, so that the children faced each other and had a jolly old sing song.'

When the war ended in 1945 the school children were invited to a Christmas party arranged by the Canadian troops which was held in the Marlborough Lines gymnasium.

'We were treated to a film show and then sat down to tea. I can also recall that we were all introduced to Father Christmas and each child was handed a toy, a bag of sweets, an orange and a bar of chocolate. Of course, during the war, sweets and chocolate were extremely scarce and could only be obtained with ration coupons.'

Teachers that Audrey remembered during her time were: Sister Marie, Sister Mary Trigg, who was replaced by Sister Patricia, Patrick Finn and Miss Gladys Hoyes.

~~~

Memories of Kevin O'Brien

On my first day in 1943 my sister Maureen was detailed to take me to school. However, on the second day she asked another, older pupil, to see me home. The older pupil failed to do so and I cried all the way home on my own.

Sister Patricia was my first teacher and taught the class to read and sing songs together. A fragment of one in particular, I can still remember "… we ride on such a bumpy bus, we jiggle in our seats", and each time the word 'jiggle' occurred we had to shake ourselves up and down. I also remember playing with a wooden tray of sand. One day in the playground I asked Sister Patricia if she would tie up my shoe laces as I had not been able to do so myself, and she willingly did this.

As my early school days were during the Second World War I was instructed by my mother and father, in the event of a German V1 weapon flying over (A rocket propelled flying bomb, commonly known as a Doodlebug) to prostrate myself face down on the ground. This occurred one morning on the way to school whilst walking along Canterbury Road, and I duly carried out this instruction when one came over at high altitude. Fortunately the device carried on in a south westerly direction.

Sister Patricia

Whenever the air raid siren went off, the whole school and teaching staff went into the air raid shelters, which were situated in the playing field at the back of the school. We held lighted candles and said the appropriate prayers for our survival.

The head teacher was Sister Marie. I subsequently became afraid of her because she had one of the pupils caned in front of the whole school assembly. This was for breaking one of the school rules that no children should climb onto the air raid shelters. It was not until many months later that I realised the great importance of such a rule, the breaking of which would greatly damage the shelter and perhaps even collapse the roof, putting the future safety of everyone at risk. In my view of this realisation, my good opinion of Sister Marie was recovered.

I well remember the unpleasant smell from the slaughter house in Peabody Road especially in the warm weather with the wind in our direction. The facility still exists today, but the odour problem does not.

The other offensive smell I well remember was when we wore our gas masks, which were issued to everyone in the event of a German gas attack. Fortunately, they were never needed, but we had to have them on constantly, and carried them to school in a special cardboard box held by a cord around our necks.

*****

POST WAR

After the war had ended, the subject of a new Secondary-modern school was raised once again in November 1946.

The Hampshire County Education Officer wrote a letter to Bishop John Henry King, stating, amongst other things, the cost of the new school: '... *calculating the cost under the Development Plan, that the cost would be £160 per school place. The cost of a new secondary school for 240 children would, therefore, be not less than £38,400 apart from the cost of the site which would of course have to be included in the capital cost.*' He also stated that: *The proposal is that the new school should be erected during the period 1953 – 1954.*

However, it wasn't until 10th December 1948 that the Hampshire County Education Officer stated: ... *I have now been able to provisionally select a site for its location at Badshot Lea in Surrey.* He then went on to say that the size of the site was *13.545 acres* ... A revised development plan was then submitted to the Education Authority by the Catholic Diocese.

The site chosen was located not far from the crossroads at Badshot Lea, Surrey, and was, by now, planned to provide: ...*that the school be a mixed two form entry Secondary-modern School accommodating 360 pupils taken from Aldershot, Ash, Badshot Lea, Camberley, Farnborough, Farnham, Fleet, Frimley and Tongham areas.* However, owing to objections by the Provincial Land Commissioner the site was rejected. Fortunately, in 1950, a larger more suitable site of 16 acres was found nearby at Weybourne, Surrey. In the meantime, owing to the financial state of affairs, four years were to slip by before the land was eventually purchased in 1954.

~~~

Ministry Regulations

The school submitted an application for a Meal Kitchen for up to eighty children. In response, the Aldershot and Farnborough Divisional Executive approved the provision of a kitchen in May 1946. Unfortunately, due to there being too few children at the school, Ministry regulations meant that a dining room was turned down. However, Sister Marie obtained permission to use the facilities at Queen's Road School for the foreseeable future.
In the meantime, it would take four more years before a meal kitchen was implemented at St. Patrick's in 1950.

~~~

With arrangements in hand for the Royal Family to visit South Africa in 1947, the school sent a letter to Buckingham Palace to which the King replied, as reported by the *Aldershot News:*

GOOD WISHES

KING'S REPLY TO FARNBOROUGH CHILDREN

The children of St. Patrick's (R.C.) School, Farnborough, are proud to have been the recipients of a message from H.M. the King on the eve of the Royal Family's departure for South Africa.

The message, dispatched from Buckingham Palace on Wednesday week, (29th. January, 1947) and received on the following morning, is as follows:-

"The Private Secretary is commanded by H.M. the King to thank the children of St. Patrick's School, South Farnborough, for their loyal assurances and message of good wishes on the occasion of their Majesties visit to South Africa. The message was the King's reply to the following letter from the school:

"The children of St. Patrick's School follow with interest the plans for your visit to South Africa. As the day of your departure approaches, we ask your Majesties and Royal Highnesses graciously to accept the assurance of our prayers that God will speed you on your way, give you a pleasant care-free journey, and bring you safely back to the Homeland after a fruitful sojourn in South Africa."

The message is signed by 99 children.

~~~

First Holy Communion 1947

Back row left to right: June Rice, Kathleen Walsh, ?, ?, Ann Rice, ?, Middle row left to right: Sister Lucia (the Superior), Sister Marie, Brian Dooner, ?, Thomas Atkins, ?, George Parker, Anthony Lynch, ?, Sister Patricia, Sister Maria. Front row left to right: Margaret Walk, ?, ?, ?, Jane Still, Teresa Staffs, ?, ?, Patricia Allen.

~~~

Teachers and pupils together in the playground

1948.

~~~

During the late 1940's concerts and Christmas Fairs were organised, of which, the proceeds went towards the school building fund. The following refers to March 1949 and was reported by the *Aldershot News*:

ST. PAT'S CHILDREN

Young people presented an attractive concert in St. Patrick's Roman Catholic School on Thursday, the festival of the school's patron saint, and every seat was occupied by an enthusiastic audience. Children of the school gave Irish songs and dances, under the direction of Sister Marie, and members of the Catholic Youth Club contributed the rest of the programme. Songs were sung by Mrs. Warburton and Mr. R. Loveder, the Wood Brothers sang and entertained at the piano, and Miss O'Brien played violin solos. A silver collection raised £13 for the School Building Fund towards the cost of the new hutted classroom.

~~~

Catholic Youth Club
Sister Marie was very well supported by the Catholic Youth Club which was organised by Fr. Marrs. Meetings were held at the school on Sundays where a debate or discussion would take place, while on Tuesday evenings a variety of social events were organised.

There was also a drama group held by Mrs. Sproule (previously of the Irish Players), who, on one occasion, were successful in winning a local completion that was organised by the British Drama League.

*****

The 1950s

Once again St. Patrick's school was experiencing problems with overcrowding and by 1950 the school managers had provided a hut, which was divided into two classrooms for the infant pupils, who were taught by Sister Patricia and Mrs. Pugh. The classroom, which was purchased from the Army, was situated at the Sherborne Road end of the school grounds.

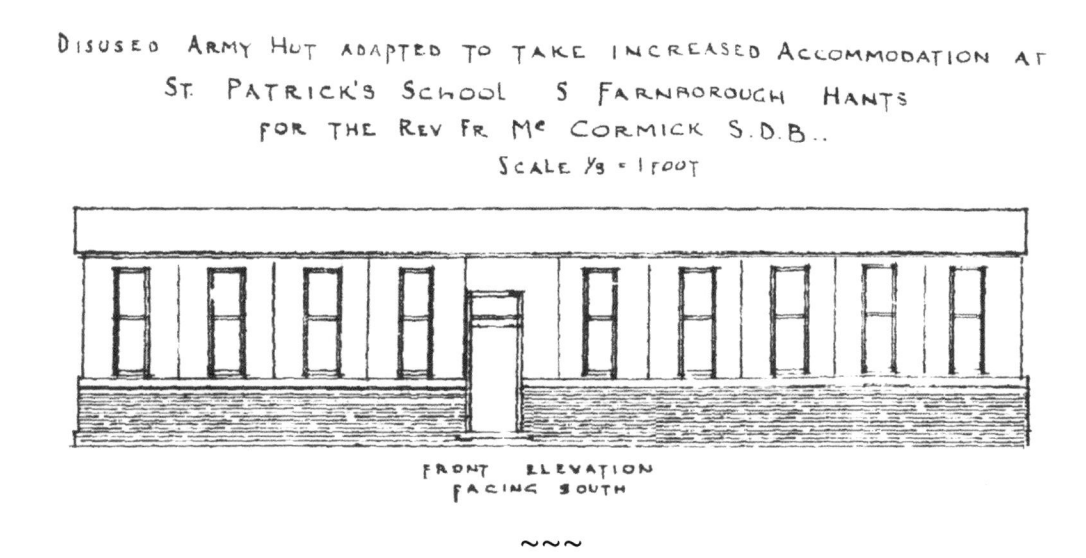

DISUSED ARMY HUT ADAPTED TO TAKE INCREASED ACCOMMODATION AT
ST. PATRICK'S SCHOOL S FARNBOROUGH HANTS
FOR THE REV FR McCORMICK S.D.B..
SCALE ⅛ = 1 FOOT

FRONT ELEVATION
FACING SOUTH

~~~

St. Patrick's School Report for 1950

His Majesty's Inspector paid a visit to the school and his report stated: *Numbers at this school have been steadily rising lately owing to the raising of the school leaving age, and to the entry of between 40 and 50 Roman Catholic children, including some from the Marlborough Lines Army School when it was handed over to the L. E. A. (Local Education Authority).*

On the first day of inspection, there were 236 on the books, but the departure of the Fair Ground children from their winter quarters reduced the figure later to 222. This increase of numbers pressing upon the original accommodation (three large rooms and one small one) has been met by utilising a temporary hut within the school grounds for 67 infants in two classes. The remaining 4 classes are housed in the main building; with one of them, class 4, it is a very tight fit.

There is at present, no mid-day meal, but when the projected wash-house is built, a container-meals service will be provided and the meal eaten in the classrooms.

The staff consists of the Head Mistress and five assistants of whom three are new to the school. There have been many changes in staff and in organisation ...

It well may be that the Managers will have either to restrict the numbers entering the school or to provide more accommodation in the near future.

The Head Mistress, who has worked very hard indeed, has had considerable difficulties over staffing with many changes that have taken place since 1945. The general level of attainment which may be said to be satisfactory at the lower end of the school is not so high in the upper reaches. At the same time, the children throughout are pleasant to meet and the oldest boys and girls show the effect of a careful training in manners and good conduct.

~~~

Mid-day Meal Service

The long-awaited washroom facility was provided in 1950, thus, at long last, enabling the school to serve hot dinners. Unfortunately, the school committee was unable to provide a hall on the school premises. The only solution was for the meals to be served in the classrooms. The plans had been approved by the Urban District Council back in 1949.

Sister Marie recalled, in July of 1950, the mid-day meals service was started, with the meals coming in containers and being served on desks in the classrooms. Washing-up took place in a lean-to scullery, built outside the main school building.

By October 1952, three classrooms in the main building were in use for 190 hungry children to have their meals. Teachers and children literally lived all afternoon in the remembrance of what had been dinner. The situation was impossible, so we gladly accepted the hospitality of South Farnborough County School and used their dinning-hall hoping that it would not rain or snow too much between noon and 1.30 p.m.

Eventually, however, Sister Marie was able to reorganise the meal service returning it back to St. Patrick's school.

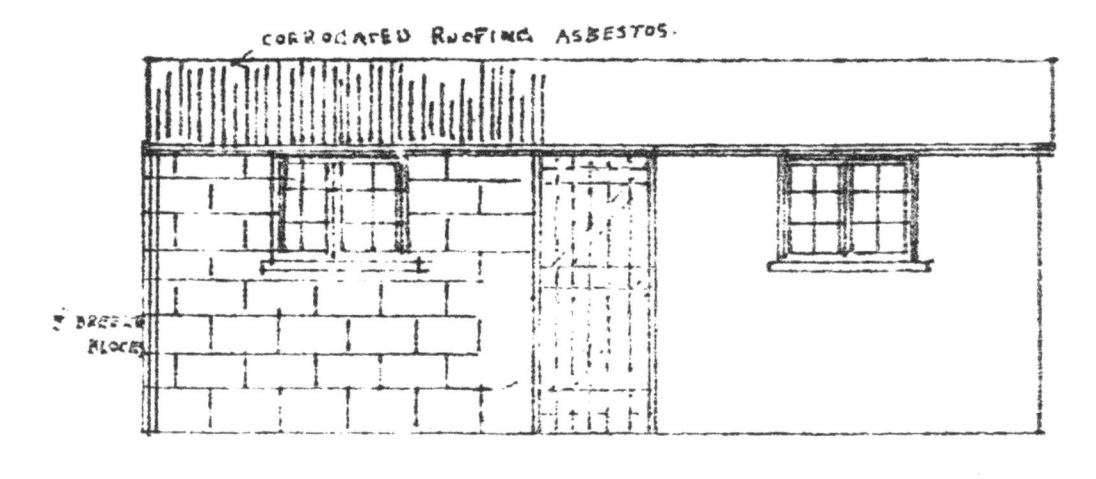

~~~

Front elevation of the new washroom, which was situated opposite to the main building

~~~

The Festival of Britain

In 1951 Sister Marie organised an outing for the senior girls to visit the Festival of Britain exhibition. Amongst those participating was Jane Still. "I remember Sister Marie making arrangements for the senior girls." she said. "However, finding that there were insufficient numbers to justify the visit, Sister Marie decided to give the 12 and 13 year old pupils the opportunity to also participate. One of the conditions was that we had to save one shilling each week towards the fare. When the day came, we had to walk from the school to Farnborough station (one and a half miles) to get the train to London. Of course, we then had to walk back from Farnborough station to the school that evening, too. However, a good time was had by one and all." she said.

The exhibition was held on the South Bank at Lambeth to celebrate Britain's recovery after the war, and to promote British architecture, science, technology and industrial design.

The 1951 Festival of Britain.

Back row: left to right: Patricia Allen, ?, Kathleen Walsh, Margaret Lambert, ?, Kathleen Parker, Elizabeth Atkins, Deidre Machin, Patricia Sheehan, Elizabeth Jones, ?, Middle row: Cecelia Green, Anne Watson, Sister Hannah, April Frances, Patricia Dunn, Amy Watson, Mary Walk, Sister Marie. Front row: Josephine O'Brian, Jane Still, Josephine Newman, Wendy Bowen, Rosemary Frances, ?, Dorothy Mc. Mann, Phyllis Wilcox.

~~~

A New Hut

In 1954 a new hutted classroom was provided by the school managers, raising the capacity to 270 children. However, by 1957 the school roll had risen to 293, and to ease the situation, it was necessary to provide another hutted-classroom bringing the total of temporary classrooms to four.

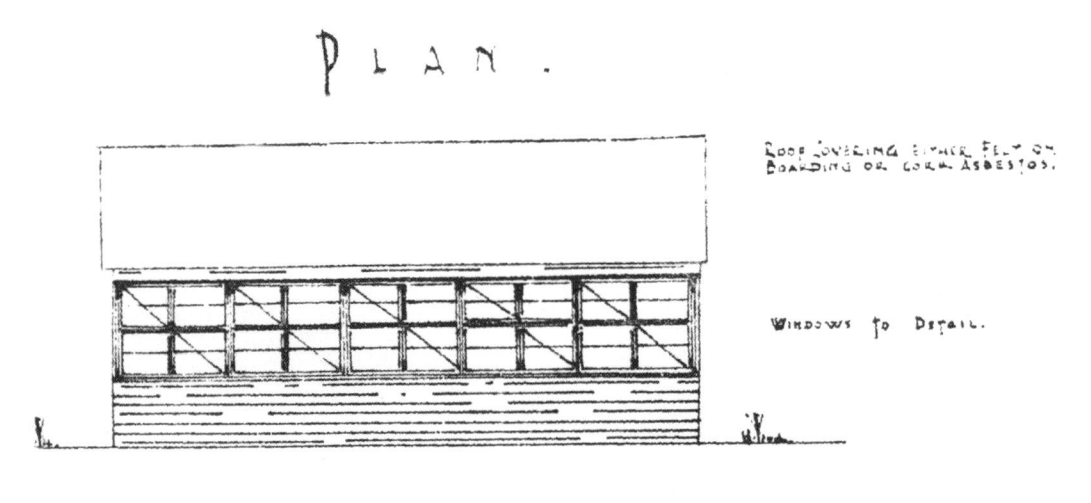

PLAN.

SIDE ELEVATION.

TEMPORARY CLASSROOM
AT ST. PATRICK'S SCHOOL
PEABODY RD. FARNBOROUGH HANTS

JULY · 1953

This hut had been purchased from Alison Brighter Homes at a cost of £614 – 7s – 0d, which, at this time, amounted to about one quarter of the cost of a newly built detached house.

~~~

Sister Marie's Memoirs

Up to 1955 I was in complete charge of the senior class, numbering 58 boys and girls between 11 and 15 years. Then I was released from full-time teaching, and was able to devote more time to the general welfare, organisation and administration of the school. I still taught music throughout the school and had three classes of English.

~~~

The Tuck Shop

Former pupil, Gretta Fearon remembers serving sweets at the school tuck shop: 'For a penny you could get either four black jacks or fruit salads and a gob-stopper was the same price and home-made ice lollies' she said, 'Winter mixtures were also available which Sister Marie would personally weigh-out. She was also well known for her cups of hot chocolate during the lunchtime period and would hold raffles. On one occasion she gave me a doll to take round to the school children, the tickets being a penny each. I would then take the doll home for the weekend and sell tickets to my neighbours in the Army quarters at North Camp.'

Stella Doona and her sister, Thelma, also served in the Tuck Shop and between them remembered selling drumsticks, bulls eyes, lucky dips, jelly babies, aniseed balls - 16 balls for a penny, chock block, a penny chew, sherbet flying saucers, and packets of love hearts. Cough-no-mores - one penny - was a small bar, ink-black, in a wrapper, that left your tongue, teeth and mouth black! Other persons they remembered serving in the shop were John Cartwright and Cathleen Warburton, but there were many more. All money raised went towards a new parish hall.

Children in front of the Tuck Shop, 1955

Back row left to right: Anthony Alden, Peter Attewell, Leslie Gallocker, Michael Grant, Anthony Walk. Third row: Carlo Colombari Terrence Botley, Frank Doherty, William Burn, ? Peter Vernon, Alice Mc. Gibbon, Stella Dooner, Vera Tracy, Joan Potterton. Second row: Wendy Bowen, Dorothy Walk, Jean Laird, Jane Still, Maureen Buckley, Margaret Warburton, Ann Ridley, Angela Smith, Moya Mc. Gowan, Isobell Butterworth, Theresa Wild, ? Front row: Eileen Hammand, Thelma Dooner, ?, Sylvia Martin, Gretta Fearon, Maureen Prendivill, Irene Fearon, Kathleen Warburton

~~~

Memories of Margaret Bartlett nee Morris

I remember playing netball for St. Patrick's; we wore blue T-shirts and green skirts. I also remember attending Sunday school; during the afternoon the Salesian Sisters would take us down to the Salesian ground at Park Road where we would play games. After the activities we would have afternoon tea from the Tuck Box. Cheese and cress sandwiches … Note: The Sunday school was also referred to by the nuns as the Oratory.

Sunday school: At the Salesian playing fields in Park Road, with the Tuck Box.

Sunday school: Outside the Pavilion at the Salesian's Park Road playing fields.

Mr. Lashley's class, 1955: Top left: Mr. Lashley. Back row left to right: ?, Vera Tracy, ? Gretta Fearon, Joan Young, Mary Doherty, Silvia Marten, Moyra Mc Gown, ?, ?. Second row: George Still, Noel Wild, Carlo Colombari, Michael Grant, Leslie Gallocker, Peter Larkcombe, Alan Stanley. Third row: Margaret Lee, Irene Fearon, Eileen Hammond, Ann James, Jacqueline Hubberstey, Thelma Dooner, ?, Gloria Gallocker, ?, Maura Kelly, Patricia Pearce, Maureen Prenderville. Front row: Trevor Dooner, Michael Cleeve, Jan Janicki, Alan Smith, David Ellerman, Daniel Girling, Alan Botley, Frank Pearce, ?, Peter Butterworth.

Mr. Lashley's main subject was Geography. However, being excellent at sport, he was put in charge of the under eleven football team, who were entered in the Aldershot and Farnborough schools league.

The under-eleven school football team, 1953/54: Back row left to right: David O'Hara, Alan Stanley, George Still, Alan Smith, Peter Larkham. Middle row left to right: Daniel Girling, Leslie Gallocker, Shaun Woods, Alan Botley. Front row left to right: Peter Jones, David Ellerman.

53

St. Patrick's School Report 10th January 1958

From the County Education Officer

The approved accommodation figure at the above school is 270 but numbers have risen considerably and last term there were 293 children on roll. To ease the overcrowding the school managers provided a hutted classroom on land adjacent to the school site. The accommodation was seen by H.M. Inspector who expressed the opinion that it would provide a suitable teaching space. In view of the fact that the School is an Aided School the managers have provided the accommodation, and the Authority will make a contribution towards the cost of heating, lighting and cleaning. The approval of the Ministry is sought to the use of this hutted classroom as additional accommodation for the School. The new classroom was brought into use as an emergency measure on 1st. November 1957.

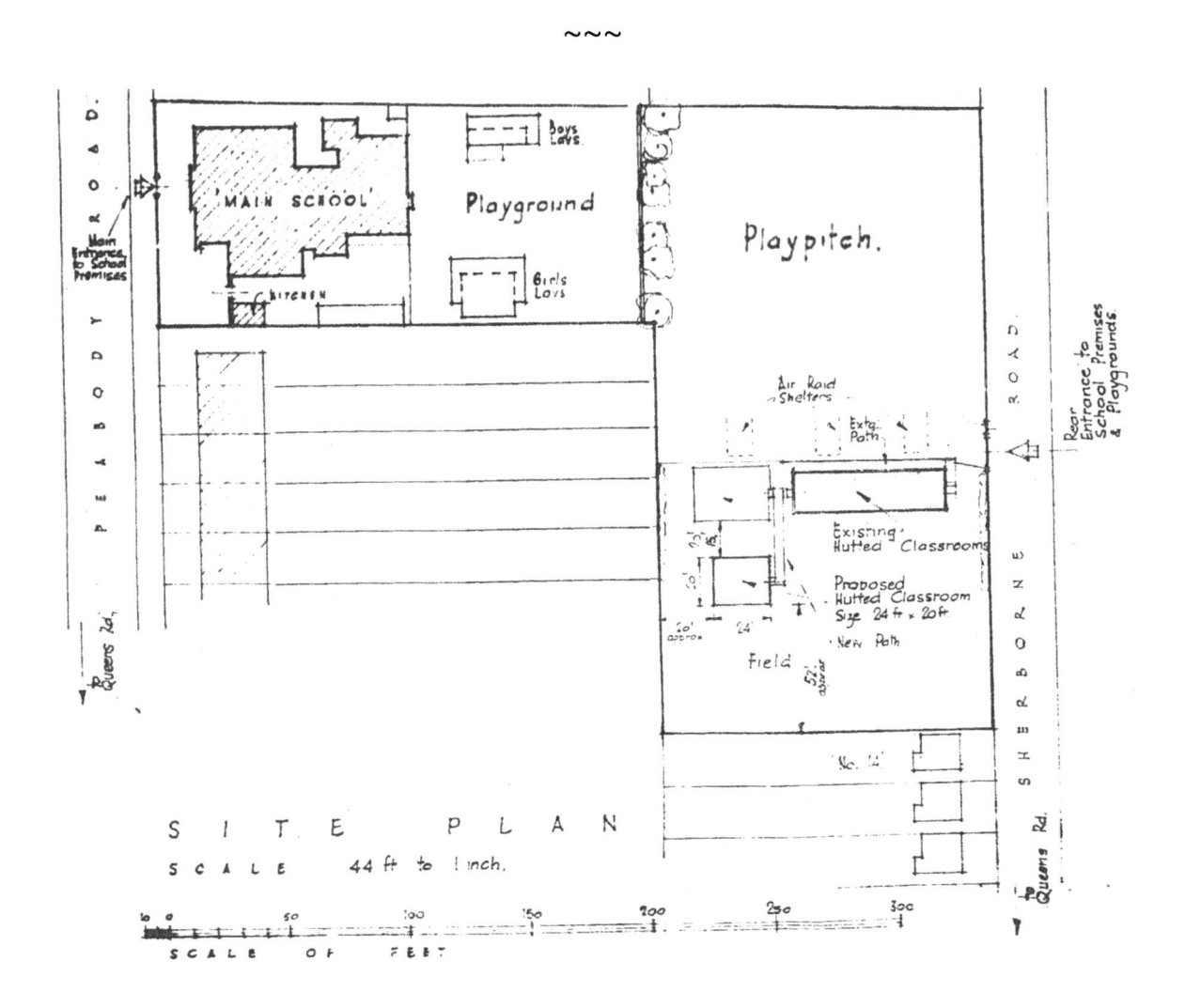

~~~

A plan of the school grounds in 1957, showing the position of the three temporary huts and also the oak trees that separated the playing areas. The outline of the three air raid shelters can be seen above the long hut.

~~~

Memories of a Former Pupil

My first teacher, whose name I can't recall, was very old and very strict! Fortunately, she was replaced by the saintly Mrs Pugh who loved every one of us. Even as an infant I already had a liking for art, but there were only seven painting easels that had to be shared. The solution, as far as Mrs Pugh was concerned, was to ask the whole class 'Who would like to paint?' Needless to say, virtually every hand in the class went up. Alas, with so few easels, I never did get an opportunity to show Mrs. Pugh just what an artist I was!

In class two, Sister Patricia introduced us to musical instruments, for instance, the tambourine, triangle and cymbals which we all enjoyed. However, behind the classroom was a lush field of green grass, which we were forbidden to venture on! But on one of those, rare, hot sunny day, she would make an exception to the rule. Needless to say, we all went wild!

In class three, Mrs. Birch, with the annual Parents' Day in mind, decided we would sing the song 'Drink to Me Only'. Sadly, it being a lament, the whole class seemed to struggle with it, much to her annoyance! Miss Birch also introduced us to Biology: we were all told to bring in a jam jar to which Miss Birch provided beans, to demonstrate just how easily they grew.

Miss Kiennan, who supervised Joan of Arc House, came to me one day and asked me if I would compete in the 100 yards sprint on the annual Sports Day. She was a lovely person and, though I dreaded the thought, I readily agreed. On the day, I lined up with runners of all shapes and sizes, desperately hoping that I might come at least a creditable third. The pistol fired and away I went, giving it my best. Alas, all I could see was the rest of the competitors in front of me! I came in sixth, and was gutted! Head down, I went over and apologised to her. Though she thanked me, I could see how disappointed she was.

As you all remember, there was a Merit system in place: a silver star for good work and a gold star excellence. Sister Marie kept a chart for each class with everyone's name on it and, from time to time, she would bring it out for all the class to see which house had the most stars. And, yes, you'll be surprised, when I tell you that I did get some stars. I even remember Sister Marie being amazed that I'd actually got some, and she went on to tell me so. Needless to say, I was quite chuffed …

In 1958, aged 11, I became a senior pupil and joined Mr. Lashley's class. From then on each year, school trips were arranged. Well I loved coach trips, and waited with bated breath as to the destination. However, my heart sank when he announced it was a visit to Huntley & Palmer's biscuit factory at Reading. But it was a day out, and I saw for the first time what it was like for people who worked in a large factory; lots of machinery and a lot of biscuits, and I well remember the 'Iced Gems' being swiftly carried along their way to the oven. On our departure, we were all given a box of biscuits to take home with us. Novel.

The second of Mr. Lasley's outings was much more interesting, it being a visit to both the Science and Natural History Museums in London - the first in the morning, followed by the second in the afternoon. Again he gave us full reign to go and explore all the wonderful things that these two museums possessed. Exciting!

The last of Mr. Lashley's outings was to the Ideal Home Exhibition at Olympia. Once more he gave us free rein and a group of us wandered the vast arena with little interest in new houses; the latest in newly fashioned interiors or the latest mod-cons. No, for some reason, it didn't quite hit the mark, and we wandered aimlessly around like lost sheep!

While in Mr. Lashley's class, the annual Parents' Day came round, and, believe it or not, he had just the thing for us! We would perform a play: *Blood on My Fish Knife*. It was a comedy about a group of people gossiping while queuing to get into a cinema. Of course we all had to learn our lines, which we practiced in the classroom. There were quite a few of us and Mr. Lashley had us all strung-out around the edge of the classroom, the queue slowly moving forward, while at the same time getting shorter and shorter. Amazingly on the day, with hearts in mouth, we all performed perfectly to loud applause.

When I moved up to Mr. Powel's class, outings took on a new dimension. His first trip was an eclectic mix of venues starting at Stonehenge. Back in those days, you could wander around and get close up to the stones; touch them and study them. But that was just the start. Our journey continued on to Old Sarum where the remains of a Norman Castle and original Cathedral could be explored. What fun we had there, not least because a thunderstorm erupted while the class were wandering around the grounds. At the time, I was at the top of the castle and, hence, got drenched running back to the coach, only to suffer Mr. Powel's derision for my endeavours. However, the sun returned and I soon dried out. Good fun. We then continued on to Salisbury to explore its magnificent Cathedral with its leaning tower, ancient clock and gothic architecture; what a wonderful sight to behold. Amazing.
There was still one more place to visit: Salisbury's agricultural show. I noted that Mr. Powel was very interested in this venue, he leaving us all to our own ends! We must be growing up! Novel. Needless to say, we waited with baited breath for his next outing.

About a year later that day eventually dawned, and we were not disappointed. Calmly and collectively, Mr. Powel described to the class, in much detail, his proposal for our next outing. Okay, this is the one! In the morning: the Tower of London and the Crown Jewels. Terrific. In the afternoon, a boat trip on the river Thames from Tower Bridge to the Victoria and Albert and King George docks. Needless to say, everyone in the class was gob-smacked. But there were implications: The cost! Entry to the Tower together with the boat trip would be expensive. However, Mr. Powell had a plan: Everyone in the class would save some money each week. And to encourage them, he announced that he would be the Banker. It worked. Everyone saved and saved until the grand day came, by which time, we even had some pocket money to spend. And what a day it was. A day none of us would ever forget. We even saw Tower Bridge open. Fantastic.   Anonymous

Mr. Lashley's class 1958

Back row left to right: Michael Reader, ?, ?, Clive Arthorn, Gerald Carver, Robert Ryan. Third row: ?, Denis Sayers, ?, Ann Addison, ?, ?, ?, ?, ?, ?, Patrick Connolly. Second row: Maureen Connolly, Isobel Mc. Mann, ?, ?, ?, ?, ?, ?, ?, ?, ?, ?. Front row: Edward Hannan, ?, ?, Earl Wilcox, Jonathan Smith, Derrick Smith, Geoffrey Hoskyns, Terrence Mullen, Edward Vernon.

*****

A New Secondary-modern

All Hallows

In May 1959, five years after the land had been purchased, work began on the new Secondary-modern school at Weybourne near Farnham. However, it would take two more years before the school was opened albeit prematurely in September 1961 at a cost of £180,000 of which a 75% Government grant was obtained from the Hampshire County Council. The remaining costs were met by four schools: St. Josephs, Aldershot, St. Patrick's, Farnborough, St. Polycarp's, Farnham, and St. Tarcisius, Camberley. (St. Patrick's contribution was £11,000, which was raised by the School Development fund.) All senior pupils from these four schools were sent to attend the new school.

The School having been named All Hallows (All Saints) had the capacity to house four hundred and fifty pupils in twenty two classrooms and an assembly hall that could accommodate them all along with a stage that was large enough to put on a show.

There were dedicated classrooms for specialist subjects, for instance: science, metal work, wood work, art and craft, domestic science and music. A library was also incorporated giving pupils additional time to study.

Note: Where St. Patrick's was concerned, it was a far cry from the days when girls were sent to Queens Road School, Farnborough, to learn Domestic Science while the boys travelled by bus to attend woodwork lessons in Aldershot.

When it came to physical education, there was a magnificent gymnasium along with the necessary showers.

The school could also boast a large playground, beyond which, were up to six acres of playing fields. All in all, the school was set for a successful future.

All Hallows from above

The main entrance to the school

The Opening of All Hallows ~ A Former Pupil Remembers

On the unofficial Opening Day of All Hallows School in 1961, groups of pupils from the various schools across the two counties arrived in great numbers, many of whom were feeling anxious as to what to expect from the new regime. Those from St. Patrick's, of course, were aware that Mr. Lashley would be teaching at the school; but what of the other teachers? Everyone had to wait and see. Needless to say, during break times, children from each and every school tended to huddle together in their own individual group.

But they needn't have worried. Our new Head Master, Mr Doyle, proved more than adequate for the task. He was very dynamic and strict, and could be seen marching around the premises organising every event that needed attention, his gown bellowing out behind him like Superman. He knew what he wanted. And we knew what to expect!

From the very first day there was a shortage of classrooms because building work was still being carried out. This meant that, from time to time, it was necessary to move a class that had been occupying perhaps, say, the art room, and relocate it to one of the science labs at the other end of the building. Well, as you can imagine, science wasn't on the agenda that year. But at least those pupils occupying the laboratories got to see what a science lab looked like! The laboratory desks, as you know, are far higher than normal desks and were novel in that the pupils had to perch on stools all day. Ouch! However, one good thing was that most of the classrooms had a nice view across the playing fields and beyond.

All Hallows was officially opened in September 1962 and all pupils that had left the school the previous July received an invitation to return to the school for the 'Official Opening'. Those who attended were presented with a prize on the day, while those not able to attend had their prize sent to them by post.

Anonymous

*****

The Infants and Juniors

St. Patrick's remained open for infant and junior pupils during which time Sister Marie was able to reorganise the school into seven classes, three for the infants and four for the juniors. She also managed to build up a collection of books which, together with those borrowed from the County Library were kept on trollies and distributed to classrooms when needed.

At this time a school magazine was produced providing news of old pupils, together with original contributions, reports on school games and additions to the library. A recorder group and dramatic society had also been formed.

In this classroom view, the original 1890 arched entrance can be seen to the right.

In July 1962 an inspection of the Peabody Road premises had been carried out by the Hampshire Education Authority. Its report stated: ... *"the premises of the above school are sub-standard in every respect and it is not possible to enlarge the site to conform with the Ministry's regulations."*

The building at Peabody Road continued to deteriorate adding to Sister Marie's burden as she tried to cope with leaking water and a broken-down heating system.

During this time the school roll had risen to 318 children, the majority of which were housed in cramped conditions. It was imperative, therefore, that a new site had to be found as soon as possible.

The same classroom showing the folding partition.

Note: Both Photographs have been taken from behind the teacher's desk.

~~~

The Transition of the School

It must have been a blessing to all those involved with the old school when in August 1962 the property of Whitefriars, a large bungalow-style building in Avenue Road, came onto the market. It had previously been in use as a private preparatory school for girls and boys who would eventually go on to attend either the Hillside Convent or the Salesian College. The grounds were situated in a plot of 4 acres with planning permission to expand over the forthcoming years.

The Salesian Fathers were quick to respond: In conjunction with Hampshire Education Authority, a compulsory purchase was arranged and the premises were purchased in January 1963 for an undisclosed fee. Needless to say there was a great deal of work to be done on the buildings: alterations and extensions had to be carried out and a new assembly hall had to be constructed. The overall costs for this work, including a £20,000 grant from the Ministry, amounted to £45,750. It would take over two years to complete the first phase, having only sufficient space for the junior pupils to attend. The new school would eventually open in June 1965.

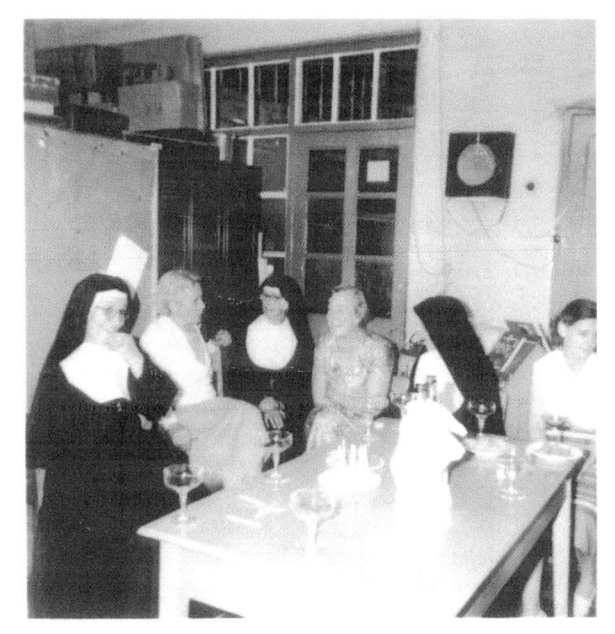

When the new school opened, Sister Marie was appointed Headmistress of both schools and, hence, it was necessary for her to commute between the two on a regular basis. However, her main concern was for the infants at the Peabody Road School, whom she put into three separate classes: they were taught by Sister Agnes, Sister Hillary, Sister Madeline and Sister Mary Edith.

By 1968 the new school was ready to accommodate the infants all of whom started there in November. What such joy it must have been for Sister Marie now that, at long last, she had all the pupils under one roof.

Teachers and Staff at Peabody Road School, 1965

Teachers and staff celebrate the opening of the new Avenue Road School on the 1st of July. Left to right: Sister Marie, Mrs. Porter, unknown, Mrs. Cartwright, the school secretary, unknown, unknown.

*****

The New St. Patricks

Memories of Theresa Loader, nee Reed

I think I joined St Patrick's School in year one, but I'm afraid I can't remember the teachers name, although I do remember the wooden huts so clearly, including the little stove in the middle where we hung our bottle green woolly tights to dry in the long winter of 1962. I loved the rows of wooden pegs for our coats with little pictures of rainbows, flowers and cats. The reception teacher was an Indian lady who wore a sari and I clearly remember the head teacher, Sister Marie. Sister Mary Edith was my teacher in year two.

I moved to the new school in Avenue Road in year three (first year juniors) and the teacher was Mrs Porter who rode a bicycle to school. My year four teacher was wonderful, marvellous, best ever, Miss Row! She had the classroom with long steps down to the playground. My next teacher was Mrs. Vernon and from there I joined Mr. Alexander's class.

I still have my school reports from juniors, but not from the Peabody Road School.

The new assembly hall alongside the old Whitefriars bungalow.

The authorities at the school must have deliberated over the naming of the new school. Their conclusion to name it after its predecessor was certainly the right one - St Patrick effectively creating a new dawn for all the pupils.

~~~

Some years later, the old school in Peabody Road was demolished. (Date unknown)

*****

Former Teachers

The Retirement of Sister Marie Ranner

In November 1968 Sister Marie moved to the new school in Avenue Road, Farnborough. She continued teaching there until her retirement in July 1969 having completed 31 years' service at St. Patrick's. The following notes have been taken from the *Salesian Sisters' Archive, Liverpool* as a tribute to Sister Marie at the school:

As she prepared to leave St. Patrick's in 1969 the education authorities commended her on several occasions for her devotion to the school and the tremendous amount of work she had done there. The Divisional; Education Officer wrote: "You certainly deserve some rest after your most devoted and energetic work for St. Patrick's, very often in difficult circumstances ... You guided the school through the difficult times of the war years and the following years of economic difficulties ..."

A problem that never seemed to go away was the lack of space in the Peabody Rd buildings for the increasing number of children seeking a place in St. Patrick's. Sr Marie found it very hard to refuse a child. In 1964 she was officially asked by the ecclesiastical and secular Education Authorities to give an understanding not to admit any more children. She countered this by petitioning to use the parish hall for a class. This was granted but the instruction top limit of the number of children was not withdrawn.

... Sr Marie was an extremely hard worker noted one sister, and gave every minute of her time to coping with a difficult situation in the school that lacked the bare necessities.

Despite all the difficulties Sr Marie said of her years in Farnborough: "I was happy there ... I liked the children ... I liked my work."

~~~

A Tribute to Mrs. Agnes Mary Pugh

Mrs Pugh a former Army School Mistress, started at St. Patrick's in May 1945 and taught the first-year infants. She continued in this post until her retirement around 1954.

In April 2011 Mr. Lashley mentioned to a former pupil that Mrs Pugh was teaching in Malta when the war began and endured the years of bombing there from 1941 - 1943. Her three sons were in the Royal Air Force. Sadly, two were shot down and killed during action. Despite these tragedies, Mrs. Pugh had a heart of gold and hence all the children loved her.

Note: Her sons had been educated at the Salesian College.

~~~

A Tribute to Sister Patricia

Sister Patricia started at St. Patrick's at the beginning of January in 1946 and taught the second-year infants. Apart from her normal lessons, she also taught country dancing, which the children performed in the playground to the crackle of a wind-up gramophone when concerts were held. She was very popular with the children as Patricia Allen recalls: "While we were out playing skipping, Sister Patricia would often join in, turning the rope while we skipped. She would also take her turn at skipping while at the same time having to hold her habit as she jumped up and down. Of course, on occasion, Sister Marie would walk by and would show her disapproval by raising her eyebrows and giving a tut-tut"

~~~

A Tribute to Mrs. Enid Mary Florence Porter

Mrs. Porter came to England from India in 1946 and took up residence in Osborn Road, Farnborough. She began teaching at St. Patrick's in 1950, her main subjects being Maths and English. However, she was also an accomplished pianist and could often be seen playing the piano at school concerts. Mrs. Porter had survived being buried alive in the 1935 earthquake at Quetta, India (Quetta is now in Pakistan) but, sadly, her husband Philip, an employee of the Indian Civil Service, and her eldest son Malcolm both died in the catastrophe. Fortunately, her son, Peter, managed to escape.

Former pupil Theresa Loader remembers Mrs. Porter and her bicycle: 'She used to ride an old fashioned bicycle which had a basket on the front that she used for transporting the children's exercise books to and from school', she said. 'It also had a green cover over the back wheel instead of a mud guard.'

Mrs. Porter continued teaching at St. Patrick's, transferring to the new Avenue Road School in 1965.

~~~

Recollections of Mrs. Joan Vernon

Joan Vernon came to St. Patrick's in 1953 having previously taught at schools in Egypt, Palestine and South Africa. Eventually, she went on to teach at the new school in Avenue Road and in due course, was appointed Deputy Head Teacher.

Standing in for the head Mistress in the Queen's Jubilee year of 1977 she reminisced about the old school, *as reported by The Aldershot News.*

... "The teachers' staff room used to be the old vestry. We used to have to dodge the bell rope which still hung in the middle of it," she remembered.

The school's old log book dates back to the 1880s. It contains entries concerning children who were absent from school because of potato picking. "Some of them couldn't come because they had no shoes to wear," said Mrs Vernon.

School lunches were brought over in a van from the central kitchens at Aldershot. The children ate in the classrooms, their desks laid out as dining tables, complete with table cloths and cutlery.

"I remember once the van didn't arrive until mid-afternoon, it got caught in a blizzard. The children were simply starving!" said Mrs. Vernon.

And with regard to the heating system: "... in Peabody Road, we had coke boilers – the fumes from them were quite overpowering at times ..."

Mrs. Vernon's comments reveal the stark reality of just how things were, not just for the pupils but for the teachers as well, in the 1950's. There isn't an ex-teacher or pupil living who doesn't remember them well!

~~~

A Tribute to John Lashley

Mr. Lashley was educated at the Salesian College, and came to the school in 1953. He played cricket for Fleet and tennis for Aldershot, so he may have felt a little disappointment that there was no playing fields or gymnastic facilities, as such, at the school. However, his abilities were soon recognised when he was given the task of coaching the junior boys in football, cricket and baseball, which took place at the Boundary Road playing fields and was to bring success to the school just two years later.

During the 1954 – 1955 football season the team achieved a remarkable treble. Their first success was winning the Aldershot and Farnborough School's League Division B trophy, a feat in its self. They then followed that up on Easter Monday by beating Park Junior School 3 – 2 to win the District Junior Cup at the Aldershot Recreation Ground.

Finally, on the following Wednesday, the team returned once more to the same Recreation ground to defeat Queens Road School, Farnborough, 2 – 1, winning the Divisional Championship. They also finished the season undefeated.

If that wasn't enough, four of the boys from St. Patrick's were chosen to play for Farnborough against Aldershot in the Perry cup. They were: Alan Botley, David Ellerman, Peter Prendiville and Shaun Woods. Alan and Shaun were also selected to represent the Aldershot and Farnborough junior team. Shaun eventually went on to play for Hampshire schools and also played for Woking and Farnborough Town at senior level while Alan played for Woking and Guildford City.

Easter Monday: District Junior Cup winners at the Aldershot Recreation Ground, 1955.
Back row left to right: Alan Stanley, David Sexton, Daniel Girling, Shaun Woods, Alan Botley Peter Hurn. Front Row: George Still, Peter Butterworth, Peter Prendiville, Martin Woods, David Ellerman.

How proud Mr. Lashley must have been.

The under-eleven B league champions 1954/55

Back row, left to right: Peter Larkham, Alan Staley, Peter Hurn, George Butterworth, George Still, Leslie Bareham. Front row: David Elleman, Peter Prendiville, Daniel Girling, Shaun Woods, Alan Botley, Martin Woods, David Sexton.

The following year Mr. Lashley decided to field an under-thirteen intermediate team. Unfortunately, six of the original team left to attend schools elsewhere, including one whose family emigrated to Australia. He was, therefore, unable to field a complete team. Despite this set back, he continued to coach the under-elevens.

Richard Walden and Gerald Carver

During the 1957/58 football season, the Under Elevens' finished second in the Aldershot and District Schools B League. Two members of that team, Richard Walden and Gerald Carver, also represented Aldershot and Farnborough Schools who competed in the Hampshire School's Cup. The team were successful in this competition defeating Eastleigh Schools in the final 4 - 0.

At the age of eleven Richard left St. Patrick's to attend Fernhill School. After he left school, he became a professional footballer and played for Aldershot, Newport County and Farnborough Town.

Gerald left St. Patrick's to attend the Salesian College after which he went to study at Loughborough College where he gained a First Class honours D.L.C. He then returned to the Salesian College where he became a Sports Master. His interest in football continued, playing for Fleet Town, and Woking in the Isthmian League.

~~~

Recollections of Arthur Powell

Joining the staff in 1954 was Mr Powell, whose subject was history. He also supervised Physical Education for the senior pupils.

I wrote to him in 2011 and received an interesting reply. Here are some of his comments and memories that I received:

I joined the staff in September 1954 straight from college. From the first day I knew I was in for an "interesting time." I soon made friends with Mr. Lashley who I think was pleased to have another man on his side against all those women, who by and large I found, I must say, very interesting.

I have never forgotten your name. One day I was taking cricket practice down on that dirt patch below the playground. You were batting and pussy footing around and I shouted at you in exasperation "'it 'it 'ard 'oskyns." And I was immediately cautioned by Sister Marie not to drop my H's."

Dinner time was always a pain. You had to prop your desk top up ready to eat your dinner whilst I had to clear my desk to serve it. Games afternoons were something else I shall never forget. John Lashley took all the kit in his car along with Mrs. Porter to the playing field whilst I walked 150 of you in hot pursuit. I had a very able helper, a big girl called Ruby, who came from the fairground people. She led the way, stopped at every road, whilst I saw everyone across, jumped on my bike and raced up to the front again ...

Other things which stand out were: the Big Flu epidemic when there were only 40 children left in the school and only John Lashley and myself to look after them; The first Friday in the month when we all had to go to Confession on the Thursday afternoon and Mass on Friday morning; Aircraft from the Royal Aircraft Establishment shaking the windows and doors, making it impossible to hear yourself speak.

One year winter came early in October and we were all shivering but we couldn't have the heat on because the Education Authority said we must not light the boiler until the 1st. November. So we waited for Sister Marie to go to lunch and then John Lashley and I went and lit the boiler ourselves.

I have to say that I really did enjoy my six years at St. Pat's, even though for one year I had 53 in my class and when the only non-teaching time I had was on Monday morning just before lunch, we used to have a music programme on the radio called Singing Together with Mr Appleby. You all had your books, so I used to take it easy by the back wall for 20 minutes.

Mr Powell left St. Patrick's in July 1960 and went on to say in his letter to me: *I spent another six years in a similar school in Sussex and 22 years in a residential school in Kent before retiring to the seaside.*

~~~

A Tribute to Miss Patricia Kiernan

Miss. Kiernan came to St. Patrick's in the mid-50s, her subjects being English Language and Religious Knowledge. She also taught the girls in physical education and, being knowledgeable in country dancing, indulged in teaching mixed groups.

Living in Camberley, as she did, Miss Kiernan took the opportunity to leave St. Patricks during the early 1960s to go and teach at St. Tarcisius School in Camberley. In 1971 she went on to become Head Mistress at St. Gregory's, on the London Road, Camberley.

*****

School class, late 1950s

Teacher not known. Back row left to right: Michael Allan, ?, Richard Walden, Michael Mc. Mann, ?, Ann Walk, ?, ?, Rosemary Vernon, ?, Paul Allen, ?, ?, ?, Middle row: ?, ?, Bernice Botley, ?, Patricia Bedford, Janet Edwards, ?, ?, ?, Barbara Dooner, ?, Denise Cougan. Front row: Earl Wilcox, ?. Colin Foster, Michael Shaw, ?, ?, Michael Collins, ?, Anthony Rainer, Michael Hennessey.

School class, early 1960s

Teacher not known. Back row left to right: Peter Donnelly, ?, ?, Nigel Lumsden, ?, ?, ?, Christopher Woods, ?, ?, Robert Rose, ?, Third row: ?, Mary Gurr, ?, ?, ?, ?, Bernadette Hannon, Janet Curtis, ?, ?, Diane Carver, Judy Potterton, ?, ?, Second row: ?, ?, Susan Ayres, ?, Monica Reader, ?, Front row: ?, ?, ?, ?, ?, ?, Robert Shaw, Kenneth Curry, ?, Glen Simons.

*****

Bibliography

Diocese of Portsmouth Archives

A03-08	Father Francis O' Farrell's notes 1886 – 1902
A03-24	Children's Suppliart 1890
A03-2 – 03-1	Letter to Bishop John Henry King 1946
A03-1-1-0	Letter to Bishop John Henry King 1948
A03-1-0-28	Letter to Bishop John Henry King 1950

Hampshire Record Office Archives

151M71/PX5	Farnborough Parochial Committee Minuets Book 1889 – 1892
H/ED4/1/1	Log book for Elementary school teachers 1890 – 1905
H/ED4/1/17	School Salaries Book F – Z 1931 – 1938
H/ED4/1/18	School Salaries Book A – F 1939 – 1946
H/ED4/1/20	School Salaries Book A – F 1945 – 1953
H/ED1/5/139	Farnborough Education Advisory Committee document
H/ED1/5/144	Farnborough RC School files 1935 – 1945

National Archives Kew

ED21/6392	School Plans 1891, accommodation figures 1910, School Report 1917
ED21/29389	Attendance Figures 1916 – 1929, School Reports 1926, 1928, 1932, 1950, 1958, 1963, Building approval and accommodation figures 1933
ED161/6600	School Report 1962

Books and Magazines

Catholic Directory.	Burns, Oakes & Co.
Come and Live Longer at Farnborough.	St. Michael's Abbey Press
Directory for Aldershot, Farnborough and District.	John Drew (Printers) Ltd.
The Lamp Magazine.	Burns, Oakes & Co.
The Story of a House: Dorothy A. Mostyn.	St. Michael's Abbey Press

Newspaper Publications

Aldershot News
Catholic Herald
Sheldrakes Military Gazette

Census

British Census 1881   St. Winifred's Convent School

****